S0-BCG-996

Government,
GOD
and
Freedom

Roger,

in freedom,

Sheriff Mack

Other books by the authors:

Judevar (western fiction)
Timothy Robert Walters

Surviving the Second Civil War: the Land Rights Battle . . . and How To Win It
Timothy Robert Walters

From My Cold Dead Fingers: Why America Needs Guns!
Richard I. Mack
Timothy Robert Walters

All titles available through Rawhide Western Publishing.

Government, GOD and Freedom
A Fundamental Trinity

Timothy Robert Walters
Richard I. Mack

 RAWHIDE
WESTERN
PUBLISHING

Safford, Arizona

THIS BOOK IS COPYRIGHT 1995
BY TIMOTHY ROBERT WALTERS AND RICHARD I. MACK
ALL RIGHTS RESERVED.
NO PART OF THIS BOOK MAY BE REPRODUCED IN ANY
FORM OR BY ANY MEANS ELECTRONIC OR MECHANICAL,
INCLUDING INFORMATION STORAGE AND RETRIEVAL
SYSTEMS, WITHOUT WRITTEN CONSENT FROM THE
PUBLISHER, EXCEPT FOR BRIEF QUOTATIONS CONTAINED
IN CRITICAL ARTICLES AND REVIEWS, AND SIMILAR BRIEF
PASSAGES IN OTHER WORKS PROPERLY ANNOTATED
AND/OR CONTAINING BIBLIOGRAPHIC CREDIT.

First Edition: Published by Rawhide Western Publishing, May 1995.

Cover design by Renee Anthony Agency
Cover photography by Dale Holladay

Typeset text in Times New Roman, titles in Arrus Blk BT,
on Intel Computers by Rawhide Western Publishing, PO Box 327,
Safford, Arizona 85548. Phone 520-428-5956. Fax 520-428-7010.

Printed in the United States of America . . . the Land of Freedom and
Unalienable Rights.

Walters, Timothy Robert, 1945
Mack, Richard I., 1952
          Government, God and freedom : a fundamental trinity
America / Timothy Robert Walters, Richard I. Mack. — 1st ed.

          Includes bibliographical references and index.

          ISBN 0-9641935-2-3 : $12.95

          Library of Congress Catalog Card Number : 95-68658

Acknowledgments

Without God and family
this book would not have been possible. Supporters and contributors to the project are too many to mention individually. Each one, however, played an integral role, and the effort would have been diminished by the absence of any player. Some team leaders were:

> Dr. and Mrs. Mark Cottrell
> Glen Dowdle
> Pastor Robbin MacDonald
> Barbara Stailey
> Phyllis Schlafly

Blessed are those who have kept the records for posterity, that we may benefit from their work. The names and works of many unwitting contributors appear in the bibliography section of this book. It is a list of highly recommended reading.

A debt of eternal gratitude is owed those who went before—a few dozen brave men who dedicated their fortunes and their lives to the founding of a new Republic, and the thousands who have died preserving it.

✝✝✝

I pledge Allegiance to the Flag
of the United States of America,
and to the Republic for which it stands,
one Nation under God,
indivisible,
with Liberty and Justice for all.

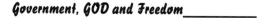

Dedication:

For the 54 brave and dedicated men who gave their signatures to the Declaration of Independence. So fierce was their commitment to the cause of freedom that they willingly risked their fortunes, their families, their *lives,* for its rightful place in the creation of a new Christian nation.

And ye shall know the truth,
and the truth shall make you free.

John 8:32

Contents

II: Religious Perspective

Prelude

"One Nation
Under God"

The Word "indivisible" has
not always appeared within our nation's Pledge of
Allegiance; it was inserted some time after the official
"pledge" was adopted. The phrase "one nation under God,"
however, has always been there. It was written as the
natural affirmation of God's guidance throughout several
centuries of history prior and subsequent to the founding of
America's unique form of Christian-based republican
government. Any American citizen so arrogant and
presumptuous as to suggest the Declaration of
Independence, the Constitution and the Bill of Rights have
somehow become antiquated, that society has evolved
beyond those inspired guidelines—that divine influence is no

longer applicable—should also believe that *air* is antiquated, and humankind should start looking for something else to *breathe*.

The monstrous problems of crime, drug abuse, violence and mainstream politics are evidence that our country has strayed way off course. The answers to those and other societal problems of today will not be found by charting new paths, but by returning to the path established by our Founding Fathers. We, as a republic, must return and never stray from the fundamental principles of liberty with which we were " . . . *endowed by* [our] *Creator*." Principles of freedom do not change with time, nor because our cities have grown larger.

Our right to freedom comes only from God. How can freedom be secured and protected if we forget or ignore the Creator who gave us liberty in the first place?

A piece of propaganda pervasive in our country is the perceived separation of church and state. Politicians and the media commonly quote a so-called constitutional requirement for the "separation of church and state." That proclamation is not found anywhere in the U.S. Constitution.

The Constitution does make two references to religion. One requires governmental officials to be bound by oath to support the Constitution (. . . *no religious test shall ever be required.*), and the other, that " . . . *Congress shall make no law respecting an establishment of religion, or prohibiting the free exercise thereof.*"

How could any reasonable person possibly construe

those two constitutional references to religion to include a requirement for separating religious principles from government? To the contrary, W. Cleon Skousen points out in his book *The Making of America*, "The founders of the constitution wanted it clearly understood that the universal, self-evident truths of religion were fundamental to the whole structure of the American system."

It should not be forgotten that the Founding Fathers believed religious precepts and morality were cornerstones of our free government. Samuel Adams warned, "Neither the wisest constitution nor the wisest laws will secure the liberty of a people whose manners are universally corrupt."

It is wholly impossible to separate the principles of freedom from the principles of religion. The God who gave us life also gave us liberty. The Founders of this great country were inspired by Him to form our Constitution. President George Washington said in his farewell address, "Of all the dispositions and habits which lead to political prosperity, religion and morality are indispensable supports."

The First Amendment warning to government to not make a "*law respecting an establishment of religion, or prohibiting the free exercise thereof*" was intended to prohibit a recurrence of King George III's state church in which colonists were forced to pay tithes (taxes), and to prohibit placing one denomination over another. The forces of good and evil have always been at war with each other. Is there a deliberate effort underway to turn us off the intended path of morality and freedom by promoting a myth that the U.S. Constitution requires a separation of church and state?

Daniel Webster described the Founders' traditional goal when he spoke at the New York Historical Society on February 22, 1852:

> *Unborn ages and visions of glory crowd upon my soul, the realization of all which, however, is in the hands and good pleasure of almighty God; but, under His divine blessing, it will be dependent on the character and virtues of ourselves and of our posterity . . . If we and they shall live always in the fear of God, and shall respect His commandments . . . we may have the highest hopes of the future fortunes of our country . . . It will have no decline or fall. It will go on prospering . . . But if we and our posterity reject religious instruction and authority, violate the rules of eternal justice, trifle with the injunctions of morality, and recklessly destroy the political constitution which holds us together, no man can tell how sudden a catastrophe may overwhelm us, that shall bury all our glory in profound obscurity. Should that catastrophe happen, let it have no history! Let the horrible narrative never be written!*

Sadly and finally, if modern American "leadership" fails to recognize that all their millions of laws, regulations, taxes and other governmental meddling are pushing our country farther off the charted course, and if we as citizens do not *demand* a return to fundamental beliefs in God —morality and freedom—then the "horrible narrative" is already being written.

Edited from final chapter of:
From My Cold Dead Fingers:
Why America Needs Guns
by Richard I. Mack
and Timothy Robert Walters
(1994)

. . . let no more be heard of confidence in man, but bind him down from mischief by the chains of the Constitution.

Thomas Jefferson

Preface

*S*ince the very beginning, humankind has had rules and instructions to live by. God told our first parents Adam and Eve, "Multiply and replenish the Earth." He commanded and further admonished them not to partake of the "forbidden fruit." What is most important here is that God left the *choice* to Adam and Eve; they were *free* to choose for themselves.

Life is a gift from God. *Living* it is based on His plan for us. Life is not without purpose any more than the creation of the universe was accidental. It is all part of the Master's plan, based on eternal principles. Besides life itself, God's greatest gift to His children is the gift of free agency—the power to choose for oneself.

This book was written to and for all Americans: Jews, Gentiles, Protestants, Catholics, Mormons, Muslims, Buddhists, atheists, agnostics, and all races and peoples—to *every* American, that we will indeed become "one nation under God."

This is without question a religious book because

freedom has always been and will always be a religious issue. There can be no freedom of religion without freedom in government, and there can be no freedom in government without freedom of religion. Indeed, the spirit of freedom *is* the spirit of God!

The work herein addresses much about government —how our republican system was designed, how it was intended to function, and where it has come. It also considers some religious beliefs and theologies as they relate to philosophies of freedom and the mechanics of government. Some emphasis will be given to the doctrines of the Church of Jesus Christ of Latter-day Saints because L.D.S. (Mormon) theology is based on the principle of free agency. Other Christian concepts will be shared in support of constitutional freedom.

Crime, violence, hatred and prejudice are all symptoms of evil. They are not the products of political and economic decay, as often argued in the halls of government, but the results of moral and spiritual decay, as recognized within the house of God. Healing the ills of contemporary America will not come as the result of political or economic strategies, but by moral and spiritual renovation.

Patrick Henry declared in 1775: "This is no time for ceremony. The question . . . is one of awful moment to this country. Should I keep back my opinions at such time through fear of giving offense, I should consider myself guilty of treason towards my country, and of an act of disloyalty towards my country, and of an act of disloyalty towards the majesty of heaven, which I revere above all things."

More than 220 years of history have not affected the timeliness of Patrick Henry's words. During a new time "of awful moment to this country," this book offers truths *and* opinions, all at the risk of "giving offense." It proclaims a loyalty to this great country surpassed in reverence only by loyalty "towards the majesty of heaven."

While it *will* explain the religious nature of liberty, it *will not* attempt to convert the reader to a specific religion. *It will, however, attempt to convert the reader to the Constitution.*

Richard I. Mack

The accumulation of all powers, legislative, executive, and judiciary, in the same hands, whether of one, a few, or many . . . may just ly be pronounced the very definition of tyranny.

James Madison

Introduction

Bill Clinton's rise to
the U.S. Presidency in 1992 brought more arrogance and corruption to federal government in this country than any assemblage of bureaucrats since the Warren Harding Administration fell apart in 1923. While there were significant differences between the two presidents, there were striking similarities in their administrations.

Harding never really wanted to be president. He was guided through a successful campaign by powerful political "friends" and an ambitious wife—most of whom saw his weaknesses as a means to their own advantage. Clinton, on the other hand, wanted to be president more than anything in the world. He, too, was guided through a successful campaign by powerful political friends and an ambitious wife—*all* of whom saw his weaknesses as a means to their own advantage.

Harding surrounded himself with personal friends at

cabinet-level positions, but mostly due to his lack of leadership skills and an inability to say no. Clinton moved his cronies into strategic positions of power with a cunning not so different from that of an underworld godfather. Harding, a conservative Republican, and Clinton, a New-Age Democrat, saw their respective administrations plagued with scandals, cover-ups, forced resignations, and the suspicious deaths of some key associates.

Harding himself died of a sudden strange stomach disorder in August of 1923. His wife burned many of his papers and letters, and refused to allow an autopsy on his body. Several of Harding's cabinet members (and closest friends) were convicted of bribery and other offenses in trials that finally ended in 1931.

Sadly for Warren Gamaliel Harding's political legacy, the mainstream media had no more compassion for conservatives during the 1920s than they did when friends of Richard Nixon broke into the Watergate Hotel. The Elk Hills and Teapot Dome scandals became widely publicized, as did the criminal trials of Secretary of the Interior Albert B. Fall and Attorney General Harry M. Daugherty. Self-serving bureaucrats were carved like pot roast by the vitriolic pens of unforgiving journalists. No evidence was ever found linking Harding to any wrongdoing, but his legacy would remain forever scarred.

Bill Clinton, from the beginning, enjoyed a journalistic shield from exposure of his questionable financial manipulations and drug connections while serving as Governor of Arkansas. "Whitewater" and "Mena" were mentioned in apologetic tones of disdain, without the accusatory barbs applied to "Watergate" and "Iran-Contra" during previous Republican administrations. Many revelations of Clinton's habitual womanizing, silenced by payoffs and costly favors, went virtually ignored by the press. He was a president cloaked in nearly impenetrable major media favor.

Grassroots America, however, was not fooled. Never before had a U.S. president inspired such passionate animosities from the citizenry of the nation. In defense of sovereignty and fundamental freedom, hundreds of citizens' militia groups sprang up around the country. Ours became a nation of Constitution defenders. The midterm elections of 1994 produced an historic Republican sweep of the U.S. Senate and House of Representatives, governors' offices and state legislatures across the country. The depth of bitterness toward Clinton was displayed in repeated hostile assaults on the White House itself. America was angry. Americans feeling the sting of betrayal—however labeled as "radical" and "deranged" by the media—were willing to sacrifice their lives and liberty in overt opposition to a president they recognized as a despot.

Why?

In the seven-plus decades since Harding's Administration, something terrible had happened. This country suffered an epidemic deterioration of its moral fiber. School curricula altered or eliminated the presence of constitutional history. Prayer was removed from classrooms and school functions. Strong ties between God, country and youth disintegrated. Dissidents became heroes. Moral degeneracy became fashionable. Future leaders of the nation, castigating all things traditional, began embracing the concepts of Marxism while espousing the virtues of promiscuity and experimental drugs.

Like a bloated carcass in a sea of societal degradation, a president from this mold was bound to eventually float to the surface. Bill Clinton, whether by design or by orchestrated maneuvering, became the chosen one. The event, however, will be credited in the annals of history as a turning point from widespread voter apathy to American activism, from blissful ignorance to elevated political awareness—from a steep downward spiraling of social mores to a renewal of spiritual commitment. When Bill Clinton was elected to the Office of President, he was coincidentally selected (by an unknowing public) as a lamb to be sacrificed on the Altar of Political Decency.

The tough assignment of restoring proper government in this country will run many years into the future. The burden will lay heavy upon those forging paths back to constitutional basics. They may or may not be successful. As forthcoming chapters in this book plainly illustrate, only a clear understanding and unequivocal embracing of the Founding Fathers' convictions in God, as relating to governmental structure, will get the job done. The task will require the efforts of *all* remaining free Americans.

Timothy Robert Walters

I:

Political Perspective

The God who gave us life gave us liberty at the same time . . .

Thomas Jefferson

Chapter One

Foundation for Freedom

An early recorded commitment to divine guidance in American government came more than 150 years prior to the penning of the Declaration of Independence. The Mayflower Compact—drawn by courageous Hollanders aboard the pioneering vessel in November of 1620—pledged an allegiance to God in the formulation of their future government:

> *In the name of God, Amen. We whose names are underwritten, the loyall subjects of our dread soveraigne Lord, King James . . . haveing undertaken, for the glorie of God, and advancement of the Christian faith, and honour of our king & countrie, a voyage to plant the first colonie in the*

Northerne parts of Virginia, doe by these presents solemnly & mutualy in the presence of God, and one another, covenant & combine our selves togeather into a civill body politick, for our better ordering & preservation & furtherance of the ends aforesaid . . .

Fewer than 20 years later, the pilgrims proved true to their convictions when a constitution of governance was prepared for some fledgling settlements of their new land. The Fundamental Orders of Connecticut—the first constitution known to history that would *create* a government—began reverently:

Forasmuch as it hath pleased the Allmighty God by the wise disposition of his divyne providence so to Order and dispose of things that we the Inhabitants and Residents of Windsor, Harford and Wethersfield are now cohabiting and dwelling in and uppon the River of Conectecotte and the Lands thereunto adjoyneing; And well knowing where a people are gathered togather the word of God requires that to mayntayne the peace and union of such a people there should be an orderly and decent Government established according to God . . .

It could be no other way.
Men of God are directed by God in the ways of their

lives. Their successes (and failures) are attributed to His wisdom. Their fears and uncertainties are offered up for His assurance and guidance. An endeavor as monumental as searching out a new land a fourth of the way around an unfamiliar world and establishing a government upon it would have been abandoned without unwavering faith in a Superior Being.

The same held for the generations that followed. Theirs was a society of uncertainties—what dangers lurked in the carving of new trails? what enemies waited to strike without warning? what malady might wipe out a family or borough? who would become the victims of fire, flood or outlaws? Not everyone had neighbors for support. Not every community was blessed with wise leadership or capable defense. Friendly and cautious Indians sometimes became hostile. Highwaymen chose helpless travelers for their easy pickings. Husbands and fathers often died young. There were few certainties.

But there was one—an undeniable belief in God. Prayer preceded every activity and event. Prayer bound families together, and provided the courage to explore uncharted paths. A firm conviction that the Creator of mankind had predetermined their destinies as the founders and settlers of a new land was the same conviction that prompted their prayers for guidance and strength and wisdom and safety and good health and successful crops. Why, then, would their commitment to a Supreme Being be put aside, or somehow disallowed, during the formulation of their government?

It would not.

Thirteen years *before* the Mayflower Compact the First Charter of Virginia proclaimed:

> *. . . their desires for the Futherance of so noble a Work, which may, by the Providence of Almighty God, hereafter tend to the Glory of His Divine Majesty . . .*

The pilgrims at Jamestown were not writing of a king, governor, emperor, dictator, or any other mortal ruler of men. Without shame or reticence, they placed their destinies in the hands of their Creator.

Throughout the 17th century, the political evolution of the fledgling colonies included references to (and reliances upon) the certainty of Supreme guidance. The Charter of Maryland (1632) called upon " . . . *God's holy and true Christian Religion . . .* " In 1639, the Fundamental Articles of New Haven described the meeting that was called for "free planters" to assemble and better " . . . *discerne the minde of God and to agree accordingly concerning the establishment of civill order . . .* "

The New England Confederation, drawn in 1643, stated unequivocally, " . . . *we all came into these parts of America . . . namely, to advance the Kingdome of our Lord Jesus Christ, and to enjoy the liberties of the Gospel . . .* " This document first united the colonies in an oath of dependence on God for their mutual well-being:

> *The said united Colonies for themselves,*
> *and for their posterities doe joyntly and severally*
> *hereby enter into a firm and perpetuall league of*
> *friendship and amity, for offence and defence,*
> *mutuall advice and succour, upon all just*
> *occasions, both for preserving and propagating the*
> *truth, and liberties of the Gospel, and for their own*
> *safety, and wellfare . . .*

These were all momentous declarations, milestones in the charting of political history. The Maryland Toleration Act, the Rights of Colonists, the Declaration of the Causes and Necessity of Taking Up Arms, and others, preceded the greatest religious document of all—the Declaration of Independence. These papers all provided the foundations (and blueprints) for the civil freedoms of speech and religion, and other "unalienable rights" as ultimately defined in the United States Constitution. Every collection of words, every assemblage of thoughts, prepared by the first pilgrims and all the later generations of colonists, with respect to establishing civil order and government, expressed gratitude, allegiance and dependence to God.

The statesmen involved in forging the new general (federal) government just over 200 years ago freely acknowledged the value and necessity of Providence. John Adams, who signed the Declaration of Independence and later became the nation's second president, wrote in a diary in February of 1765:

> *I always consider the settlement of America with reverence and wonder, as the opening of a grand scheme and design in Providence . . .*

Adams never dreamed his private reflections would become public record. He wrote the words simply because he believed them. Ten years later, in a private letter to his wife, he reiterated his convictions:

> *Statesmen may plan and speculate for Liberty, but it is Religion and Morality alone which can establish the principles upon which Freedom can securely stand.*

Benjamin Franklin said, "Providence seems by every means intent on making us a great people."

The sentiment was a common thread binding the colonists together in a formidable unit of strength. Nowhere was it written better than by Alexander Hamilton in a patriotic pamphlet in 1775—the year preceding the Declaration of Independence:

> *The Sacred Rights of Mankind are not to be rummaged for among old parchments and musty records. They are written, as with a sunbeam, in the whole volume of human nature, by the Hand of the Divinity itself, and can never be erased or obscured by mortal power.*

In 1777, there occurred a shortage of Bibles in the colonies. The Continental Congress assigned a committee to study the matter. The committee recommended congressional action because " . . . *the use of the Bible is so universal and its importance so great . . .* " The Congress subsequently ordered 20,000 Bibles imported from Holland and Scotland for distribution to the various states. Four years later a second shortage prompted the Congress to approve the first American printing of the "Bible of the Revolution." (Any such moves today would be met with howls of protest over First Amendment interpretations. Not to worry, though, because no contemporary congress would risk taking such a stand.)

Thomas Jefferson's single reference to "a wall of separation between church and state" was an idea totally separate and apart from the *union* that existed between government and God. The Founding Fathers believed in anything *but* a "separation" as interpreted by modern courts. The phrase never appeared within the Declaration of Independence or the U.S. Constitution. The First Amendment in the Bill of Rights said simply: "*Congress shall make no law respecting an establishment of religion, or prohibiting the free exercise thereof . . .* "

It could not have been written more plainly. It means two things—the government shall not establish its own church, and citizens are free to practice whatever religion they choose. It does not say restrictions will be imposed on prayer in schools, invocations at commencement exercises, or the word "God" appearing in the Boy Scouts' oath. It might well be remembered at this time that the Bill of Rights was not drawn to place restrictions on the people of the nation, or on the several states; it was meant to place restrictions on the federal government *only*. Therefore, the changing interpretations of constitutional clauses that restrict personal religious activity (including prayer in school) are clear violations of individual unalienable rights.

James Madison, a Framer of the Constitution and fourth President of the U.S., said: "There is not a shadow of right in the general government to intermeddle with religion . . . This subject is, for the honor of America, perfectly free and unshackled. The government has no jurisdiction over it."

In 1785, Madison penned his acclaimed *Memorial and Remonstrance*, within which he ranked religious duty even above civil obligations:

> *We hold it for a fundamental and undeniable truth "that Religion of the duty which we owe our Creator and the manner of discharging it, can be directed only by reason and conviction, not by force or violence." . . . It is the duty of every man to render to the Creator such homage and such only as he believes to be acceptable to him. This duty is precedent, both in order of time and in degree of obligation, to the claims of Civil Society. . . . We maintain, therefore, that in matters of religion, no man's right is abridged by the institution of civil society, and that religion is*

wholly exempt from its cognizance.

It was this very concept that spawned the American Experiment. No government had ever been established in the world that gave credit to man's Creator for man's rights and freedom. The concept produced a unique upside-down pyramid of authority in which the Almighty Creator granted "certain unalienable rights" to the people, who in turn established a government with very limited power. In most other civilizations and societies, the government itself was recognized as the "almighty" entity that granted (and withheld) the rights of the people at whim and will. A great deal has been written—especially during the 20th century—to undermine the Christian foundation of America, but one must only examine the documents of record to recognize these efforts as the work of anti-Christian revisionists.

A government founded on the principled belief that people are " . . . *endowed by their Creator with certain unalienable rights . . .* " demanded a set of established (however unique) priorities. What are those unalienable rights? What is their order of importance? The U.S. Constitution, based wholly on the religious foundation provided by the Declaration of Independence, was written to define and protect the individual rights to life, liberty and property—in that order. The Constitution was not drawn to *grant* the rights of citizens, but to *protect* them. The Founding Fathers, inspired by the natural laws of God, were effectively structuring a government the likes of which had never been seen upon the earth before.

Again, men of God are directed by God in the ways of their lives. The denominational affiliations of the Founding Fathers may have varied—Methodist, Baptist, Presbyterian—but their common inspiration was their strong faith in a Supreme Being. Much of the virtue and morality instilled into this "government wrought by God" has since been allowed to erode, not unlike a granite mountain forever lashed by wind and rain. The basic foundation may remain in place, but the outstanding features have been altered, providing a less resistant surface for the abrasive elements that demand change.

Special interest groups of many different creeds have used and abused the U.S. Constitution, demanding specialized interpretations that serve their own designs and purposes. A perverted judicial system has seen fit to meet their demands. The First Amendment now protects pornography and desecration of the flag, and simultaneously forbids children to pray at school. It's ludicrous to suggest these were the visions of the Founding Fathers when they sought freedom of speech and protection from a state-run church. Ours is a government envied by most other nations in the world. Many countries tried to imitate it in the closing years of the 20th century when the failures of their own socialistic and communistic systems seemed imminent. And yet there is within this government a cancer eating voraciously at its vital parts—a malignancy fed by the ignorance of lawmakers, the blind empowerment of judges, and by the evil selfishness of greedy and power-driven executive leaders.

The United States government has only worked because of the insightful crafting of a one-of-a-kind blueprint for freedom as inspired by the law of God. It has been written and repeated that never was there, before or since, an assembly of men charged with so great and arduous a trust, whose motives were more pure, or whose commitment was more exclusively and anxiously devoted to the task before them, than were the members of the Constitutional Convention of 1787. But the men themselves gave credit to the Almighty.

James Madison summed up the sentiments of all:

> *We have staked the whole future of American civilization, not upon the power of government, far from it. We have staked the future of all of our political institutions upon the capacity of each and all of us to govern ourselves, to control ourselves, to sustain ourselves according to the Ten Commandments of God.*

So why have we strayed so far from the concept?

Because government 200 years after ratification of the Constitution was no longer based on the Constitution as it was inspired, written and intended; it was based on perverted courtroom interpretations by appointed jurists, either conservative or liberal, who had removed God from the equation.

In the last half of the 20th century bureaucratic visionaries attacked the tenets of the Constitution with a vengeance. The Federal Government granted itself more and more authority. Congress and various presidents authorized agencies with the "power" to set policy as enforceable as *law*. Federal lawmakers flung legislation about like wrecking balls demolishing the sovereign rights of states and private citizens. Thousands of special-interest lobbyists swarmed over Washington, virtually unnoticed for a couple of decades, making life very sweet for the politicians who favored them. Marxist liberals honed their philosophical scalpels for the task of excising capitalist values from the American system of enterprise. Schools stopped teaching anything about the Constitution. The Supreme Court ordained itself as the ultimate lawmaking body from which there was no appeal.

The result of this unchecked burgeoning of federal authority was exactly as the Founding Fathers had feared it would be. Exorbitant taxes consumed the earnings of private citizens. The runaway "generosity" of legislated entitlements made dependents (slaves) of millions of Americans. The rights of property owners became meaningless. Usurpation of states' rights was the rule rather than the inadvertent exception. Freedom to choose and practice religion was decided by dogmatic judges or federal agents with heavy artillery. Law-abiding citizens were made into criminals by the imposition of unconstitutional laws passed by "elected" officials arrogantly claiming to "know what is best" for the people—even against the will of the people.

The Constitution, fortified by the Bill of Rights, was written expressly to prevent these kinds of abuses of power. Nonetheless, the worst nightmares of the Founding Fathers had come true during the 40 years preceding 1994 (an uninterrupted era of left-wing control in Congress). One of the last true scholars of the Constitution to serve in a high federal office was Ezra Taft Benson—religious leader, author, dedicated statesman, selfless human being, and Secretary of Agriculture under President Dwight Eisenhower. As the country entered the final decade of the 20th century, battle lines were being drawn between a large segment of the citizenry demanding a return to constitutional basics and New Age visionaries pushing for allegiance to One World Government.

If the visionaries prevail, individual rights and liberties as Americans have known them under the U.S. Constitution will cease to exist. Private property will become communitarian property. The free enterprise system will succumb to socialism. The "subjects" of the nations will be slaves to the Government, living on rationed entitlements. The American Experiment will have died. One World Government will be the embodiment of all the failed political systems previously inspired by man.

Again, government as established under the United States Constitution was not inspired by man. The American democratic Republic was unique in its concept that men created equal were " . . . *endowed by their Creator with*

certain unalienable rights . . . " It was—and still is—the
only government of its kind in the world.

George Washington, in his first Inaugural Address,
April 30, 1789, said:

> *. . . it would be peculiarly improper to omit
> in this first official act my fervent supplications to
> that Almighty Being who rules over the universe,
> who presides in the councils of nations, and whose
> providential aids can supply every human defect,
> that His benediction may consecrate to the liberties
> and happiness of the people of the United States a
> Government instituted by themselves for these
> purposes . . . No people can be bound to
> acknowledge and adore the Invisible Hand which
> conducts the affairs of men more than those of the
> United States.*

Erosion of freedoms and constitutional rights in this
country has been hastened by a *loss* of acknowledgment and
adoration for the "Invisible Hand." The only hope for a
restoration of constitutional basics and guaranteed
unalienable rights is a return to the social, moral and
religious principles of our Founding Fathers. The real
foundation for freedom is not within government itself, but
within the Creator who gave it.

No human laws are of any validity, if contrary to [the law of nature]*: and such of them as are valid derive all their force . . . from this original.*

Sir William Blackstone

Our constitution was made for a moral and religious people; it is wholly inadequate for any other.

John Adams

Chapter Two:

The Concept
of Natural Law

Most American

citizens can recite from the Declaration of Independence the passage concerning Creator-endowed unalienable rights. However, in the opening lines of that inspired document, even preceding the most familiar of quotable quotes, Thomas Jefferson drew upon " . . . *the Laws of Nature and of Nature's God . . .* " to justify the colonists' desire for independence. Contained within the body of the document are references not only to "God's Nature" and the "Creator," but to "Divine Providence" and "Supreme Judge of the World."

The Founding Fathers realized that wisdom beyond

the limits of mortal man was necessary to preserve liberty. Even a unique and perfect government as envisioned by the revolutionaries would not be spared the weaknesses of humankind without the influence of a Spiritual Being. That's why "Natural Law" became the root and foundation of the entire American Experiment.

In the hearts and minds of those who wrote the Declaration of Independence and framed the U.S. Constitution, "Natural Law" was synonymous with "God's Law." It was the Golden Rule, the Ten Commandments, Right Over Wrong, Good Over Evil—the incarnation of virtue and morality. It was *not* a discretionary ingredient. It existed without question or debate.

It was Natural Law.

Remember, unalienable rights as endowed by the Creator consist of three fundamental elements—the right to life, the right to personal liberty, and the right to private property. In putting together a limited general government to secure these elements for themselves and their posterity, the Founders relied on three basic precepts: one, that natural law and unalienable rights were granted by the Creator; two, that a written constitution would ensure a government of just laws rather than arbitrary rulers; and, three, that virtue and morality among God-fearing people of the nation would provide the best defense against tyranny.

The people of Boston adopted The Rights of Colonists at a town meeting in 1772, proclaiming their natural individual (moral) sovereignty:

> *Among the Natural Rights of the Colonists are these first. a Right to life; Secondly to liberty; thirdly to Property; together with the Right to support and defend them in the best manner they can—Those are evident Branches of, rather than deductions from the Duty of Self Preservation, commonly called the first Law of Nature—*

> *. . . The natural liberty of man is to be free from any superior power on earth, and not to be under the will or legislative authority of man; but only to have the law of nature for his rule . . .*

Pope Leo XIII, who died in 1903, believed that all fair and just civil laws " . . . derive from the law of nature their binding force." He added, "The authority of the divine law adds its sanction."

Others who did not participate in the framing of the Constitution have recognized the importance of natural law. Joseph Cook, a 19th century American lecturer, stated:

> *A natural law is a process, not a power; it is a method of operation, not an operator. A natural law, without God behind it, is no more than a glove without a hand in it.*

Natural Law—God's Law, i.e., *moral* law—is the steadfast foundation for the American republican form of government. Scholars and statesmen have reaffirmed that premise through the centuries, as did noted clergyman and author of the late 1800s, H. J. Van Dyke:

> *No matter what theory of the origin of government you adopt, if you follow it out to its legitimate conclusions it will bring you face to face with the moral law.*

Nearly a century later, U.S. Secretary of State John Foster Dulles reiterated:

> *Our nation was founded as an experiment in human liberty. Its institutions reflect the belief of our founders that men had their origin and destiny in God; that they were endowed by Him with inalienable rights and had duties prescribed by moral law, and that human institutions ought primarily to help men develop their God-given possibilities.*

The necessity for natural law was borne in a conviction among the Founding Fathers that although certain unalienable rights were endowed by the Creator, there was no guarantee of protection or sustainability of those rights within human society unless there existed a code of law on a scale higher than the station of mortal man. Therefore, Natural Law—or God's Law—was accepted as the supreme guarantee of unalienable human rights, and was so named in the Declaration of Independence.

While the American experiment of government rooted in Christianity was unique, the concept of natural law was not. Cicero, the Roman statesman and orator who lived before the birth of Christ, wrote:

> *Law is the highest reason, implanted in Nature, which commands what ought to be done and forbids the opposite. This reason, when firmly fixed and fully developed in the human mind, is Law.*

He added that law is intelligence " . . . *whose natural function it is to command right conduct and forbid wrongdoing* . . . " Cicero heralded God as the source of supreme law.

"Natural law" was never mentioned in the Constitution, but it was an integral part of the rationale of its framers. And why shouldn't it have been? The primary works of Cicero were commonly taught as basic texts in the grammar schools of English-speaking nations during the 18th century. Thomas Jefferson and John Adams, James Madison and George Washington, Hamilton, Franklin, and most of the several dozen statesmen who crafted and signed the two most important founding documents of this nation's organization, were schooled as youngsters in the principles of Natural Law. The concept was as recognized and accepted as the principles of Christianity—the two of which cannot be separated.

The concept of natural law explains easily why the

written Constitution is so brief (as compared to the rambling, and seemingly endless, charters of some other nations in the world). The U.S. Constitution, while never mentioning natural law, is the embodiment of an *unwritten* constitution based on the Christian morals and beliefs pointed up in the Declaration of Independence, and fostered in the hearts of the courageous compatriots who were embarking on the grandest political journey of all time.

Supporting Cicero's teachings, many more scholars and philosophers subscribed to the tenets of Natural Law— Polybius, Montesquieu, John Locke, Sir William Blackstone. Drawing upon the resource of their collective wisdom and knowledge, the Founding Fathers were able to sculpt a form of government more unique and enduring than any other conceived by man. The American Republic became politically unstable only when 20th century visionaries began to corrupt it with philosophies contrary to Christian principles.

The last half of the 20th century saw the American system of government injected with heavy doses of secular humanism (paganism)—socialistic legislation, anti-Christian court decisions, allegiance to world organizations, government by greed and corruption, atheistic interpretations of the Constitution and Bill of Rights. The same time period saw powerful bureaucracies bullying the sovereign citizens of states, runaway taxation, skyrocketing crime rates, a dogmatic judicial system encouraging social and moral decay. There was loss of prayer in schools, the deterioration of education, the promotion of deviant lifestyles and the epidemic spread of social diseases—all of which seriously impair the God-given rights to personal security (life), personal liberty and private property.

Unalienable rights—even when endowed by the Creator—remain "unalienable" only as long as they are protected (guaranteed) by Natural Law.

*Walters ~ Mack*_____

No people can be bound to acknowledge and adore the invisible hand which conducts the affairs of men more than the people of the United States.

George Washington

Chapter Three:

The Separation Folly

The separation of church and state is a classic example of the U.S. Supreme Court acting as Supreme Legislator of the Land. This is not a Court interpretation of law because there is no law. Neither does the Constitution mention a "separation of church and state." It says only that " . . . *no religious test shall ever be required . . .* " for government officials to serve. The First Amendment promises that "*Congress shall make no law respecting an establishment of religion, or prohibiting the free exercise thereof . . .* "

It was simple—and simply understood by the colonists. They did not want the United States Government to establish or administer a state church, as King George III had done in England. And they did not want the free exercise of religion prohibited or restricted in any way—which is exactly what our modern Supreme Court has done over the issue of free prayer in schools. James Madison, often called the "Father of the Constitution," stated very precisely, "There is not a shadow of right in the general government to intermeddle with religion. Its least interference with it would be a most flagrant usurpation."

How, then, did the U.S. Supreme Court become the last authority over when and where " . . . *the free exercise thereof* . . . " is acceptable? The Founding Fathers made it ubiquitously clear in their writings, their addresses, the example of their daily lives, that no government intervention, interruption or "intermeddling" into the free exercise of religion would be tolerated.

John Adams said in 1787 that the American people should be taught in school "every kind of knowledge that can be of use to them in the practice of their moral duties, as men, citizens, and Christians, and of their political and civil duties, as members of society and freemen." In the same breath he coupled religion and government as subjects to be ingrained in the hearts and minds of students in a new and free nation.

The Constitution does not say anything about education, but the Founders believed institutional learning was an integral ingredient in the preservation of liberty. George Washington and James Madison advocated establishing a university dedicated to preparing young people solely for the task of defending and perpetuating

American liberties. Other Founding Fathers—Franklin, Adams, Jefferson, James Wilson, John Dickinson—wrote adamantly about the need for citizens schooled in the theory and practice of government to sustain the new Republic. These were the same men who established the new American government on eternal Christian principles. The separation of church and state, as imposed upon 20th century Americans, had no place in their design for freedom.

Dr. Benjamin Rush, a Pennsylvania scholar who signed the Declaration of Independence, believed that formal education should be receptive to religion *and* liberty. In his home state Rush proposed a plan for institutional learning in which curricula for schools included history, languages, economics, math and chemistry, military science, the principles of legislation, and Christian doctrines as taken from the Bible itself. Again, government and religion were treated as married and inseparable.

The first textbook printed in the U.S. was a small book called *The New England Primer*. It was the equivalent of a "first grade reader" at a time when there was no distinction between grade levels. All students entering the American system of schools from 1690 to very near 1900 began learning to read and write from the *Primer*. It taught the alphabet and how to form and connect syllables into words. Most interesting are the exercises presented to help children apply what they had learned. Each letter of the alphabet introduced a sentence for the child to read:

A wise son maketh a glad father, but a foolish son is the heaviness of his mother;

Better is a little with the fear of the Lord, than great treasure and trouble therewith;

Come unto Christ all ye that labor and are heavy laden and He will give you rest;

Do not the abominable thing which I hate, saith the Lord;

Except a man be born again, he cannot see the kingdom of God;

. . . and so on.

The letters "V" and "Z" were omitted. Otherwise, every letter preceded a *biblical verse!* This was a textbook—and probably the most important textbook in the American school system—for more than 200 years. Practice questions in the back of the book also related directly to the Bible:

What's the fifth commandment?
What's forbidden in the fifth commandment?
What's required in the sixth commandment?
What's forbidden in the sixth commandment?

Some four decades following complete ratification and implementation of the Constitution and Bill of Rights, French jurist and author Alexis de Tocqueville visited the new American Republic and traveled throughout the colonized states, observing for himself the Great Experiment in motion. He subsequently wrote *Democracy in America*—one of the most detailed and insightful studies of early American culture and politics ever published. On religion and government, de Tocqueville related:

> *On my arrival in the United States the religious aspect of the country was the first thing that struck my attention; and the longer I stayed there, the more I perceived the great political consequences resulting from this new state of things.*
>
> *Religion in America takes no direct part in the government of society, but it must be regarded as the first of their political institutions . . .*

With respect to the role of religion in schools during the period of de Tocqueville's observation, he wrote:

> *. . . every citizen receives the elementary notions of human knowledge; he is taught, moreover, the doctrines and the evidences of his religion, the history of his country, and the leading features of the Constitution.*

Would the Supreme Court of the 20th century have us to believe that the entire nation, from its beginning, was violating the Constitution until a panel of esteemed and enlightened justices saved us all from ourselves in the early 1960s? The Founding Fathers must have known what they themselves intended the relationship between religion and government to be. Indeed, they did. And they spelled it all out very concisely in Article VI and the First Amendment. Those who read more into these passages than what they say are guilty of violating the very clauses they are trying to interpret.

It's easy to see how far from the Founders' original beliefs and concepts, intentions and applications, we have come. It is far more difficult to understand why.

Ezra Taft Benson, wearing the hat of a former Cabinet secretary as well as that of a constitutional scholar, said there are a couple of reasons for the erosion of our rights and freedoms. In his 1986 work *The Constitution: A Heavenly Banner*, Benson said we can credit government with allowing federal agencies the growth and assumed power to regulate and control millions of citizens. Even more crippling is the abandonment of fundamental principles by the U.S. Supreme Court. In giving examples to fortify his assessment, Benson specifically named "the area of morality and religion." Then he wrote:

> . . . *it is apparent that the republican form of government established by our noble forefathers cannot long endure once fundamental principles*

are abandoned. Momentum is gathering for another conflict—a repetition of the crisis of two hundred years ago. This collision of ideas is worldwide. Another monumental moment is soon to be born. The issue is the same that precipitated the great premortal conflict—will men be free to determine their own course of action or must they be coerced?

Benson's logic is this: a cornerstone of freedom was kicked from the foundation of American government by the Court's liberal rulings in religious matters. The connection he makes between Christian principles and American liberty cannot be overlooked. The importance of religious influence cannot be denied. This assessment was written by a man who understood and served the republican form of government, one who knew and loved the Constitution—and it was written two and a half decades after the Supreme Court began embracing the tenets of atheism.

The Court has claimed the "wall of separation between church and state" was built by Thomas Jefferson—that his intent was their mandate. Nothing could be further from the truth. The phrase never appeared in the Declaration of Independence, the U.S. Constitution, the Bill of Rights, or any other document of the fledgling government. In 1802, Jefferson wrote the phrase in a letter to the Danbury Baptist Association of Connecticut in an effort to explain why he would not proclaim a day of national thanksgiving:

> *Believing with you that religion is a matter which is solely between man and his God, that he owes account to none other for his faith or his worship, that the legislative powers of government reach actions only, and not opinions, I contemplate with sovereign reverence the act of the whole American people which declared that their legislature should "make no law respecting an establishment of religion, or prohibiting the free exercise thereof," thus building a wall of separation between Church and State . . .*

Jefferson simply believed that proclaiming a day of national thanksgiving might somehow resemble an " . . . *establishment of religion . . .* " There are many documented examples of other actions by Jefferson, however, that illustrate his acceptance of a strong relationship between church and state. As President, he encouraged the Senate to ratify a treaty that would help set up a church among the Kaskaskia Indians. In the Virginia Legislature, he wrote a bill for establishing elementary schools in which he stated religious readings must be consistent with the tenets of all religious sects and denominations. As president of the University of Virginia, he supported inviting major denominations "to establish their religious schools on the confines of the University."

Thomas Jefferson did not foster any perception of a "wall between church and state" as interpreted and applied by the Supreme Court since 1962—nor did any other of the several dozen Founding Fathers. Evidence to the contrary is overwhelming. Why would Jefferson, if in fact he believed no relationship should exist between God and government, write with his own pen " . . . *the Laws of Nature and of Nature's God . . .* " within the Declaration of Independence? Why would he appeal (in the same document) to the " . . . *Supreme Judge of the World . . .* " and declare " . . . *a firm reliance on the protection of Divine Providence . . .?*"

Does the Court's perceived "wall between church and state" allow for certain exceptions? How do we explain otherwise the inscription of the Bible passage from Leviticus 25:10—"*Proclaim Liberty throughout the land to all inhabitants thereof*"—appearing on Philadelphia's Liberty Bell? How do we justify the reverse side of the Great Seal of the United States, adopted by the Continental Congress in 1782, emblazoned with the Latin motto, "*ANNUIT COEPTIS*," which means, "He (God) Hath Favored Our Undertaking?"

Why does every session of the U.S. House and Senate begin with prayer if it is unconstitutional in public schools? Why does each house of the legislature have its own chaplain? Are we to believe there are no conflicting religious precepts among more than 500 lawmakers on Capitol Hill, but there might be among 30 students in a classroom?

The declaration "*In God We Trust*" appears in a picture in the rotunda of the U.S. Capitol building, on the sail of the first pilgrims' ship. The phrase was later used in the lyrics of the *National Anthem*, by Francis Scott Key. It became an inscription on U.S. coins during the Civil War. Congress ordered it printed on all coins and paper money in 1955, and a year later it was congressionally designated as the official U.S. national motto. All this from a government that insists there can be no relationship between itself and God.

If a true "wall" exists between church and state, then why must couples obtain licenses from the state before being married by a priest or minister? And why are those marriages recognized? Why do courtroom witnesses swear upon Bibles that their testimony will be true? Why do elected officials seal their oaths with the words "So help me God?" Why are churches listed as §501(3)(c) nonprofit entities with the Internal Revenue Service and then *taxed* for their holdings? Churches should be answerable only to God, not to the I.R.S., if the Supreme Court is right.

The biggest example of hypocrisy exists within the Supreme Court itself. Each session of the Court opens with the crier pleading, "God save the United States and the Honorable Court!" Over the head of the Chief Justice, the Ten Commandments decorates the wall. *This* is the unit of government that will not let kids pray at school!

Little wonder is it, then, that the Reverend Peter Marshall once prayed before Congress:

> *Our Father, remove from us the sophistication of our age and the skepticism that has come, like frost, to blight our faith and make it weak . . . We pray for a return of that simple faith,*

> *that old-fashioned trust in God, that made strong and great the homes of our ancestors who built this good land and who in building left us our heritage . . . Amen.*

American clergyman William Ellery Channing—a man born during the chaotic founding process—gave complete credit for the discovery, settlement, colonization and political organization of our new nation to God:

> *It was religion, which, by teaching men their near relation to God, awakened in them the consciousness of their importance as individuals. It was the struggle for religious rights, which opened their eyes to all their rights. It was resistance to religious usurpation which led men to withstand political oppression. It was religious discussion which roused the minds of all classes to free and vigorous thought. It was religion which armed the martyr and patriot in England against arbitrary power; which braced the spirits of our fathers against the perils of the ocean and wilderness, and sent them to found here the freest and most equal state on earth.*

The U.S. Supreme Court would appear to deny any acknowledgment of the Founding Fathers' convictions in Providence. These deviant attitudes of the nation's most learned men of law have detoured our nation onto a hazardous path that can only lead to total social chaos and moral degeneration. They have weakened and undermined every facet of American government, and have toyed recklessly with our Creator-endowed fundamental rights and liberties.

Sir Francis Bacon, a 17th century jurist and philosopher whose wisdom extended beyond his time, wrote:

> *When any of the four pillars of government —religion, justice, counsel, and treasure—are mainly shaken or weakened, men had need to pray for fair weather.*

The Court-imposed separation of church and state is a folly, a myth, a lie. It is a political movement the founding colonists would have taken up arms to prevent. They fought the Revolutionary War over less issue. It will take far more than a prayer for "fair weather" to rectify the wrongs and repair the damages that have been inflicted upon the most perfect system of government in the world—a government built on doctrines of God.

When men put their trust in God and in knowledge, the government of the majority is, in the end, the government of the wise and good.

William Spaulding

True religion is the foundation of society, the basis on which all true civil government rests, and from which power derives its authority, laws their efficacy, and both their sanction. If it is once shaken by contempt, the whole fabric cannot be stable or lasting.

Edmund Burke

Chapter Four:

Cancer of the Court

The Founding Fathers
left a legacy of spiritual conviction for their descendants to follow. One of them, Benjamin Franklin, summarized the "fundamental points in all sound religion" in a letter to Yale University President Ezra Stiles:

> *I believe in one God, the Creator of the universe. That he governs it by his Providence. That he ought to be worshipped. That the most acceptable service we render to him is in doing good to his other children. That the soul of man is immortal, and will be treated with justice in another life respecting its conduct in this. These I take to be the fundamental points in all sound religion.*

The "fundamental points" expressed by Franklin were:

(1) the recognition and worship of a Creator;
(2) that the Creator has issued a plan for righteous and moral living;
(3) that mankind is to be held responsible for its own interactions;
(4) that life extends beyond the mortal life of the human body; and,
(5) individuals are judged for life in the Hereafter.

These five tenets of "sound religion" were the core substance of most all the Founders' writings—especially on the topic of government. From the Christian perspective, they were occasionally referred to as the basic "religion of America." John Adams said these five fundamental beliefs were the "general principles" upon which the American civilization was founded. The Founding Fathers believed that "good government and the happiness of mankind" could prevail only as long as these basics were partners with the rudimentary teachings of knowledge and morality in the public schools.

That was 1787.

Much had changed by 1991 when officials at the Lakeview Elementary School in Norman, Oklahoma, refused to allow 11-year-old Monette Rethford to pray during school recess. Monette would take her Bible onto the playground and pray for her classmates and teachers.

She was noticed when several other students joined in. Someone complained, and the school principal told Monette that prayer was "illegal on school property." When Monette's father appealed to school officials, he too was told that his daughter's behavior was against the law. Ultimately, Monette's family filed a lawsuit to protect her constitutionally-guaranteed right to freedom of speech.

Not only was Monette Rethford's right to free speech violated by this arbitrary interpretation of the "wall of separation between church and state," but so was her freedom to practice the religion of her choice. This kind of blatant disregard for the rights of a single individual is the result of a self-righteous liberal Supreme Court gnawing away at the moral fiber of a Christian-founded nation the same way an unchecked cancer destroys its victim from within.

Let us be reminded of the First Amendment:

> *Congress shall make no law respecting an establishment of religion, or prohibiting the free exercise thereof. . .*

Having read the words and understood them for exactly what they say, it is difficult to comprehend the convoluted rationale of the Court, beginning as early as 1947 when the case of *Everson v. Board of Education* set the precedent for all future "wall of separation" interpretations and no-establishment rulings, and initiated new levels of Court usurpation of power over state governments that have never been challenged. It all came out of a New Jersey case over school districts transporting students to nonpublic schools. Justice Hugo Black, in delivering the majority opinion, said the wall of separation between church and State "must be kept high and impregnable." That doctrine of separatism has been the watchword ever since for liberals and atheists, anti-American subversives, and the Court itself.

The case of *McCollum v. Board of Education* came, then, within a year, in 1948. In that test of free religious exercise, the Court struck down a program in Illinois that allowed privately employed religious teachers to hold classes in public school settings. Although attending the religion classes was strictly voluntary, Illinois' compulsory education law was reason enough for the justices to fear that some students might be unwillingly exposed to Christian instruction. Their insidious decision prompted a whole avalanche of anti-Christian, unconstitutional rulings that could not be challenged to any higher court.

The Court effectively ended all forms of prayer in schools beginning with *Engel v. Vitale* in 1962, a case that, ironically, spiraled out of an attempt in New York to avoid controversy by introducing a nondenominational prayer:

> *Almighty God, we acknowledge our dependence upon Thee, and we beg Thy blessings upon us, our parents, our teachers, and our country.*

Although it would have satisfied Thomas Jefferson's desire for the inclusion of religious activities in school that were universally accepted and offensive to no one, the omniscient Court decided that implementing the prayer was akin to the " . . . *establishment of religion* . . . " It mattered not that students would have the options of participating, remaining silent, or even leaving the room.

In 1963, in *Abington School District v. Schempp*, the Court ruled that reading the Bible in public schools was a violation of the "establishment" clause. The decision struck down one of the last vestiges of the Founding Fathers' noble vision—a 50-year-old Pennsylvania law that required the reading of several Bible verses at the beginning of each school day. There were no comments or instruction included, only a brief reading of verses. Children were excused from participating upon parental request.

Stone v. Graham, in 1980, removed privately funded copies of the Ten Commandments from public classrooms in Kentucky. A notation on each display that the Bible verses were recognized as the "fundamental legal code of Western Civilization and the Common Law of the United States" carried no significance with the Court. Justice William Rehnquist dissented from the majority, saying, "The Court's emphasis on the religious nature of the first part of the Ten Commandments is beside the point." However, the liberal majority feared that displaying the Ten Commandments on classroom walls might somehow " . . . *induce . . . children to read, meditate upon, perhaps to venerate and obey . . .* " them.

By this time, any similarity between the original meaning and the Court's interpretation of the First Amendment had disappeared. Remember, one of the restrictions placed on the federal government by that amendment disallowed " . . . *prohibiting the free exercise thereof. . .* " And yet, discrimination by a convoluted Court has had the effect of *taking away* this most fundamental liberty.

In 1985, the Court struck down an Alabama law that allowed students to participate in a moment of silence (or meditation) at the beginning of each school day (*Wallace v. Jaffree*). Again promoting an atheistic agenda, the Court's majority agreed the state statute could not be allowed to stand because its sponsor, a state senator, had spoken to the legislative record his desire to "return voluntary prayer" to the classroom setting. Appropriately, Justice Rehnquist again criticized the Court's perception of the "wall of separation," calling it "a metaphor based on bad history, a metaphor which has proved useless as a guide to judging." He recommended the idea be "frankly and explicitly abandoned." Rehnquist drew upon a more accurate record of history to point out that President George Washington— prompted by the same body of Founders who passed the Bill of Rights—proclaimed public prayer as a way of giving thanks for the "many and signal favors of Almighty God." And he admonished finally that history itself must ultimately " . . . *judge whether it was the father of his country in 1789, or a majority of the Court today, which has strayed from the meaning of the Establishment Clause.*"

The "majority of the Court," since the 1940s, has produced a potpourri of rulings that clearly illustrate a liberal acceptance for violations of the "Free Exercise" clause. However, the first such action may have come as early as 1878 when the Court decided the federal government could make bigamy a crime, thereby " . . . *prohibiting the free exercise thereof . . .* " by Mormons practicing church-sanctioned polygamy. In that case (*Reynolds v. United States*), the Court concluded that to permit polygamy would " . . . *make the . . . doctrines of religious beliefs superior to the law of the land.*"

Recall that the Founding Fathers originally structured the general (federal) government as the smallest block at the bottom of an upside-down pyramid, with the people and then the Creator occupying the larger blocks at the top. God's law *was* the "law of the land."

Since 1940, nothing would seem further from the truth. While the Constitution was intended to ensure freedom of religion without exclusion, the nation itself was founded on Christian principles. The cancer of the Court and its demoralizing effect on the various tenets of faith are unquestionably shown in the following few examples:

1940—*Cantwell v. Connecticut*
Regarding a dispute over Jehovah's Witnesses canvassing a predominantly Catholic neighborhood, the Court determined that while the freedom to *believe* is absolute, the freedom to *act* upon that belief is not.

1940—*Minersville School District v. Gobitis*
Two Jehovah's Witness students were forced to recite the "Pledge of Allegiance," even though doing so was contrary to their religious beliefs. The decision was, however, reversed in another case (*West Virginia Board of Education v. Barnette*) three years later.

1943—*Prince v. Massachusetts*
The Court upheld a Jehovah's Witness woman's conviction on child labor law violations for allowing her young daughter to voluntarily sell literature door-to-door.

1961—*Torcaso v. Watkins*
The Court abolished a Maryland statute requiring all public officials to declare their belief in the existence of God, thereby broadening the concept of "religion" to include atheists and anti-Christian affiliations within a government founded on Creator-endowed rights.

1982—*United States v. Lee*
An Amish employer was forced to pay Social Security tax on his Amish employees, in direct conflict with the Amish faith, as the Court decided that every person "cannot be shielded from all burdens" imposed by the government. This ruling ranked "the fiscal vitality of the social security

system" above the free exercise of religion.

1986—*Goldman v. Weinberger*
The Court supported the military's need for "instinctive obedience" over individual religious freedom by refusing an ordained Jewish rabbi serving in the Air Force the right to wear his skullcap.

1986—*Bowen v. Roy*
Religious liberty fell victim to bureaucratic regulation when an Abanaki Indian lost medical benefits for his two-year-old daughter by not furnishing a Social Security number—an act he believed would "rob her spirit."

Without doubt, fundamental liberties in the arena of religion have been eroded by arbitrary judicial opinion, ignorant of the Founding Fathers' primary wishes. In the process, the Constitution itself has taken on "meanings" different from those basic guarantees contained in the Bill of Rights—sometimes meanings (interpretations) completely *opposite* the convictions of the Founders. Flawed constitutional decisions of the Court have resulted from incomplete historical research, inconclusive academic analysis, and self-asserting political bias. In turn, the negative impact on the whole of society is reflected in thousands of incidents in which the First Amendment's promise of "free exercise" has been stripped away.

Religious students have been barred from meeting on campus. Students have been forbidden from passing out religious literature before and after school. Unaffiliated evangelists have been arrested for preaching on public streets. Zoning laws have prevented individuals from holding Bible studies inside their own homes. Church schools and day care centers have been forced to submit to municipal licensing procedures. Some municipal governments have had to remove religious symbols from their official seals. School principals have refused to allow any acknowledgment of the birth of Jesus Christ in Christmas programs. Church groups have been refused the use of public parks for Easter sunrise services and other religious observances. Textbooks either negating or ignoring the significance of religion in history have been written and introduced into classrooms. Darwin's "theory of evolution" is taught as basic truth (over the objections of parents) while the Creator is ignored by order of the Court.

The Founding Fathers would have abolished an agency of the federal government guilty of imposing these effects on the lives of God-fearing Americans. Thomas Jefferson wrote:

> *Can the liberties of a nation be thought secure when we have removed their only firm basis—a conviction in the minds of the people that these liberties are . . . the gift of God? That they are not to be violated but with his wrath?*

74

Abraham Lincoln feared a too-powerful Supreme Court:

> *If the policy of the Government, upon vital questions affecting the whole people, is to be irrevocably fixed by the decisions of the Supreme Court . . .* [then] *the people will have ceased to be their own rulers, having to that extent practically resigned the Government into the hands of that eminent tribunal.*

George Washington recognized the importance of religious influence within the processes of government:

> *It is impossible to govern the world without God. He must be worse than an infidel that lacks faith, and more than wicked that has not gratitude enough to acknowledge his obligation.*

When French statesman and author Alexis de Tocqueville traveled the new American nation, observing the success of an experiment only a few decades old, he was particularly fascinated by a unique marriage between government procedures and religious principles. In his *Democracy in America,* he wrote:

> *I had almost always seen the spirit of religion and the spirit of freedom pursuing courses diametrically opposed to each other; but in*

America I found that they were intimately united, and that they reigned in common over the same country.

If de Tocqueville were to visit this nation today, his assessment of "the experiment" would read much differently. The Supreme Court, by subjective opinion, has effectively divorced God from government, and, in doing so, has dismantled the bridge between government and freedom. Americans have learned to live in fear of bureaucratic regulations, legislative usurpations, excessive taxation, and other forms of governmental tyranny. Behaving like a never-ending Constitutional Convention, the Supreme Court has pared and shaped and sculpted the contents of that founding document to support most governmental abuses of power.

Noted historian Channing Pollock once observed that most democracies of the world have lasted only about 200 years. Is the American Experiment nearing the end of its life? Some powerful socialists would like to see the United States of America enter into the 21st century as a small voice in a very large central world government. Excising religious influence from the political process is one key element in accomplishing that end.

Why?

The American Experiment was not started like any other *democracy* in the world; it began as a *republic*. Uniquely, it was based on the concept of God-given rights to liberty. Those Creator-endowed rights to life, liberty and property are the guarantee of its longevity. The experiment will die only if God is not allowed to participate in the equation.

Christianity is the basis of republican government, its bond of cohesion, and its life-giving law. More than the Magna Charta itself the Gospels are the roots of English liberty.

Richard Salter Storrs

Chapter Five:

Of Effect and Consequence

*S*omeone once outlined the five primary factors responsible for the collapse of a powerful political empire:

> *1. The undermining of the dignity and sanctity of the home, which is the basis of human society.*

> *2. Higher and higher taxes and the spending of public monies for free bread and circuses for the populace.*

3. The mad craze for pleasure, sports becoming every year more and more exciting and brutal.

4. The building of gigantic armaments when the real enemy was within the decadence of the people.

5. The decay of religion—faith fading into mere form, losing touch with life and becoming impotent to warn and guide the people.

The list bears an ominous resemblance to prevailing conditions of the 20th century that have served to undermine most all of the liberties set forth and guaranteed within the U.S. Constitution. However, the list was not written with respect to the Republic of the United States of America. It was written by Edward Gibbon in 1787—the year of the Constitutional Convention in Philadelphia—as a part of his great work *The Decline and Fall of the Roman Empire.*

Why does it sound like a description of modern American conditions? Could the Great Experiment fail for the same reasons the Roman Empire failed? American author John Steinbeck once said, "If I wanted to destroy a nation I would give it too much and I would have it on its knees, miserable, greedy and sick." How well that describes the 20th-century evolution of American society. Having grown fat since the Great Depression of the 1930s, government encouraged a reliance on entitlements (handouts). The inner-cities rotted, crime and disease spread, morals degenerated and millions learned how to be paid not to work, as big government grew bigger by creating a society of beggars cadging morsels from powerful politicians. Government of, by and for the people became a government of regulating agencies authorized by elected officials promising more and larger handouts.

Ezra Taft Benson, a bureaucrat himself who loved only his God more than his country, wrote in 1969:

> *Do you realize that a great republic, Greece, provided a great degree of freedom and a high standard of living, but it vanished. Rome came along with a great republic. Roman citizenship was cherished; yes, it was sought—it was* bought. *But Rome, falling into the throes of cheap politics, began to tax everything that could be taxed, and to regulate everything that could be regulated—even to the load that could be carried on an ass. And what was the result? Yes, they began to put names on the public payroll until a third of the citizens of Rome were on the national payroll, and that republic collapsed.*

American citizenship is certainly sought—even *bought* —by the millions of immigrants entering the country by legal and illegal paths. To "cheap politics" the American system is no stranger. The American people have too long endured the strangling effects of thousands of new laws passed each year that serve only a few and discriminate against the masses. "Good" legislation is typically burdened with self-serving amendments that ultimately lead to more taxation and regulation. And the Federal Government is bloated with a work force exceeding by several hundred times the largest private employer in the nation.

Political, social and moral decay in America can be inextricably tied to the diminished value placed on religious influence within our system. When George Washington declined to run again for the office of president, he delivered an admonition to future leaders:

> *Of all the dispositions and habits which lead to political prosperity, Religion and morality are indispensable supports. In vain would that man claim the tribute of Patriotism, who should labour to subvert these great Pillars of human happiness, these firmest props of the duties of Men and citizens. The mere Politician, equally with the pious man ought to respect and to cherish them. A volume could not trace all their connections with private and public felicity. Let it simply be asked where is the security for property, for reputation, for life, if the sense of religious obligation* desert *the oaths?*

President Washington spoke at a time when the effects of religious influence upon the founding process were still easily recalled. The sentiments of the Founding Fathers on this issue, however, represented far more than a passing popular fad. Scholars hailing from several decades on either side of the founding era in America subscribed to like philosophies, recognizing and proclaiming the importance of Christian influence on political processes.

Sir James Allen Park, an English judge who died half a century before the Continental Congress convened, wrote:

>*Christianity is mixed up with our very being and our daily life; there is not a familiar object around us which does not wear a different aspect because the light of Christian love is on it—not a law which does not owe its truth and gentleness to Christianity—not a custom which cannot be traced, in all its holy healthful parts, to the gospel.*

Henry Martin Field, an American clergyman and author who did not attain adulthood until 50 years *after* the drafting of the Constitution, observed wisely:

>*The loss of popular respect for religion is the dry rot of social institutions. The idea of God as the Creator and Father of all mankind is in the moral world, what gravitation is in the natural; it holds all together and causes them to revolve around a common center. Take this away, and men drop apart . . .*

Anti-Christian (anti-religion) decisions of the U.S. Supreme Court during the last half of the 20th century represent far more than enlightened interpretations of the Founding Fathers' work. The Court took on a highly political posture as a succession of presidents filled vacancies on the bench with appointments they believed would further their party agendas. From a political perspective, five individuals on the Court—accountable only to their own consciences—when in agreement, have the ability to change history and effectively undermine the very foundation of the system that placed them there. They become an indisputable legislative body, an omnipotent regulating agency, an unapproachable nationwide school board, the enemies of unborn children, the friends of capital criminals, the crafters of clever constitutional interpretations, and the unchallenged rulers of a nation.

There should be little misunderstanding, then, about the erosion of religious freedom in America, or the restrictions placed on " . . . *the free exercise thereof* . . . " And only since the removal of prayer and other religious activities from the instructional environment of children has the moral fiber of the nation turned spongelike, absorbing the decadence of a society schooled in the *un*importance of God.

David Barton, a meticulous researcher, author and constitutional crusader from Aledo, Texas, illustrates with the use of graphs in his book *America: To Pray or Not To Pray* a direct correlation between the absence of prayer in schools and the plagues of modern society. Barton says, "In a single day, the Supreme Court divorced this nation's schools from more than two centuries of their heritage." Perhaps the most startling thing about Barton's work is the preponderance of evidence that increased rates in student suicides, dropouts, pregnancies and sexually transmitted diseases among teens, did not develop over a long period, but rose suddenly and dramatically with the elimination of prayer from schools.

After the infamous 1962 decision (*Engel v. Vitale*) that ended prayer in public schools and effectively denied thereafter the free exercise of religion to millions of young Americans, student suicides skyrocketed by 400 percent. Suicide rates for 15- through 24-year-olds before 1962 had been relatively low and stable, but reflected steady and rapid increases every year after that for the next 15 years.

Birth rates for unwed girls ages 15 through 19 had been fewer than 15 per 1,000 girls, and had even experienced a decline just prior to 1962. After *Engel v. Vitale*, pregnancies within the same age group increased in number every year for two-and-a-half decades. Pregnancies among girls from ages ten to 14 shot up by more than 550 percent.

Coincidentally, before 1962, sexually transmitted diseases were present in fewer than 400 of every 100,000 older teens. When the influence of religious principles was removed from the classroom environment, incidents of STDs rose to 1,300 of every 100,000 in a ten-year span, up 226 percent. Cases of gonorrhea in ten- to 14-year-olds spiraled upward by 257 percent.

Premarital sexual activity in 18-year-olds increased by 208 percent within 15 years after 1962. During the same period, 17-year-olds were up 271 percent. Sixteen-year-olds—a group that had seen little fluctuation upward or downward for many years—suddenly burgeoned by 365 percent. Sexual activity among 15-year-olds, practically nonexistent before 1962, suddenly exploded by 1,000 percent. Within two decades, 30 percent of all 15-year-olds had become sexually active.

Of course, there is a very strong natural correlation between the rise in sexual activity and the increases in venereal diseases and teen pregnancies, but no stronger than the natural correlation between the advent of increased teen promiscuity and the absence of Christian influence within an important adolescent environment.

Students also experienced a negative effect scholastically when prayer was taken away from them at school. S.A.T. achievement tests were introduced into public schools in 1926. The national average for test scores never rose or declined more than two consecutive years until 1963. After the removal of prayer from classrooms, test scores declined nationally every year until 1980, and have since remained miserably low. Additionally, high school dropouts, as relating only to G.E.D. testing, increased by 1,000 percent from 1962 to 1982, and have shown no signs of improving.

Some educators, in the interest of social and scholastic self-defense, began establishing more private religious schools after 1963. Before the removal of prayer from public classrooms, Christian schools in the U.S. numbered about 1,000. Twenty years later there were 32,000! Interestingly, S.A.T. scores in private religious schools never dropped. With only about 12 percent of the nation's students attending private schools, a phenomenal 39 percent of the nation's top scholars were being generated from among them. Finally—and contrary to some arguments—those students in private religious schools received less than half the funding spent on public school students. According to the U.S. Department of Education in 1990, about $2,200 were being spent per student in private schools, as compared with $5,400 per student in the public system.

Societal decay was markedly advanced when the Supreme Court steered the nation away from the religious principles fostered in the Constitution. Violent crime statistics, virtually unchanged for more than a decade prior to 1962, ballooned by more than 800 percent in the next 30 years. Divorce rates tripled every year from 1963 to 1981. Female single-parent households grew in number three times faster than the population growth rate, and unmarried couples living together grew from one in 85 to one in 25. By the early 1990s, the U.S. was the world's leader in violent crime, divorce, voluntary abortions, illegal drug use, and the Western-world leader in teenage pregnancies and illiteracy. This from a nation graduating over 700,000 students annually unable to read their own diplomas.

This from a nation alienated from the religious principles upon which it was founded more than 200 years ago.

David Barton says the issue of prayer in schools is not a *religious* issue, but a *national* issue. He adds that when the influence of Christian principles was stripped out of the education system in America, then a new authority was created—the authority of oneself to set his or her own standards for distinguishing right from wrong, good from bad. The individual sense of morality was then allowed, like water, to find its own level, and that level has been a downstream torrent to social and moral decadence with no spiritual foundation to dam it.

The same decadence pervaded government. Thirty years after *Engel v. Vitale*, individuals schooled without the inclusion of prayer were being elected and appointed to important government positions. Others who may have experienced some religious presence in school had forsaken it for a blind acceptance of the Supreme Court-invoked "wall of separation." Only a few continued to recognize the connection between Christian philosophy and constitutional rights. It has been proved repeatedly throughout the world that government without God breeds corruption. The United States Government was never exempt from this inevitability. The last half of the 20th century saw Creator-endowed rights to life, liberty and property take a back seat to corruption, greed, scandals and epidemic usurpation of power.

In 1832, statesman and orator Daniel Webster wrote:

> *Who shall reconstruct the fabric of demolished government? Who shall rear again the well-proportioned columns of constitutional liberty? Who shall frame together the skillful architecture which unites national sovereignty with States rights, individual security, and public prosperity? No, if these columns fall, they will be destined to a mournful, a melancholy immortality. Bitterer tears, however, will flow over them, than were ever shed over the monuments of Roman or Grecian art; for they will be remnants of a more glorious edifice than Greece or Rome ever saw, the*

edifice of constitutional American liberty.

The "columns of constitutional liberty" have been weakened; they have not fallen. "States rights, individual security, and public prosperity" have been degraded, but not destroyed. The "fabric" of government has been damaged, but not yet "demolished." Therefore, in preclusion to Mr. Webster's ominous warning, the questions should be: Who can *save* the worn fabric of government from demolition? Who can *preserve* the aging columns of constitutional liberty? Who can *redraw* the delicate lines that unite national sovereignty with states' rights, individual security, and public prosperity?

It will take many years to repair the damage done. Front-line offense in the effort should include the children of the nation. Children are not born evil or corrupt; they are conditioned by society to *become* either good or bad. Ezra Taft Benson said, "The power of America lies in every boy and girl in the hinterlands of this great nation." The strength of the nation has always derived from its children—even the Founding Fathers being the product of their upbringing. We should remind ourselves often of John Adams' timeless admonition:

> *Our constitution was made for a moral and religious people; it is wholly inadequate for any other.*

How much plainer could it be?
We are missing the key ingredient of the recipe. The

Founders included it, relied upon it, and heralded its significance, because they knew it was essential to the success of the uncommon government they were forming. As this ingredient—a strong relationship with God—was deemed less and less important and removed further and further from the process, the element of uniquity was lost. The Christian-rooted American Republic began to resemble failed godless democracies from other parts of the world, and, under the administration of President Clinton, even teetered on the brink of Marxist socialism.

There must be renewed nationwide personal subscription to religious principles. The places to begin regaining that lost portion of American heritage are most naturally the public schools, and within government itself. Government "programs" cannot stem the tide of social and moral degeneration; they never have and never will. But the children of the nation, fortified with strong Christian values, can *turn* the tide of social decay, and ultimately (*eventually*) restore the strengths of morality and virtue to the Great American Experiment.

Without a remarriage of the fundamental principles of government and God, "the edifice of constitutional American liberty" will crumble, and Daniel Webster's warning will have become an epitaph.

That is the most perfect government under which a wrong to the humblest is an affront to all.

Solon

Take away a man's right to own property and you take away his right to be independent, substituting serfdom in the place of freedom.

Strom Thurmond

Chapter Six:

The
Sanctity of Property

The fight for American independence spawned from dissatisfaction over King George III's oppressive rule. The grievances of those willing to risk their fortunes and lives in the interest of freedom were spelled out clearly in the Declaration of Independence. More than two dozen specific charges aimed directly at the monarchy described " . . . *a history of repeated injuries and usurpations, all having in direct object the establishment of an absolute Tyranny over these States.*"

The colonists were tired of excessive taxation. They had grown weary of arbitrary mandates from abroad and no representative government among themselves. They were tired of epidemic human rights abuses—mock trials and extreme punishment for "pretended" offenses, the murders of citizens by British officers, invasions of their homes and confiscation of food, personal belongings and other property.

They appealed to " . . . *the Supreme Judge of the World for the rectitude* . . . " needed to absolve their allegiance to the British Crown. The Revolutionary War ultimately gained for them the independence they had so declared. A new "general government," then, was established with very limited powers under the inspired U.S. Constitution and its accompanying Bill of Rights.

Striving to prevent a recurrence of government by tyranny, the Founders stuck stubbornly to the concept of Creator-endowed unalienable rights. The very foundation of government for the United States (Colonies) of America included three principle articles:

(1) the right to personal security (life);
(2) the right to personal liberty (freedom); and,
(3) the right of private property (the pursuit of happiness).

These principles comprised the overall spectrum of "unalienable rights." A general government was designed and installed only to "secure these rights." Acknowledged as "truths to be self-evident," these rights were recognized and accepted as "endowed by their Creator."

We hold these truths to be self-evident, that all men are created equal, that they are endowed by their Creator with certain unalienable Rights, that among these are Life, Liberty and the pursuit of Happiness. That to secure these rights, Governments are instituted among Men, deriving their just powers from the consent of the governed.

No single fundamental principle of freedom was considered more important than another. Each was derived from the Creator. Therefore, the right to own property was equal to the rights to life and liberty. John Adams expressed that conviction:

The moment the idea is admitted into society that property is not as sacred as the laws of God . . . [then] anarchy and tyranny commence. Property must be secured or liberty cannot exist.

James Madison, the Father of the Constitution, declared that property, as held by any one man, was exempt from interference by government or other men under *any* circumstances:

Government . . . is not a just government, . . . nor is property secure under it, where property which a man has . . . is violated by arbitrary seizures of one class of citizens for the service of the rest.

The European system of feudalism made slaves of those who worked the land; no one ever prospered beyond the sparse handouts of the government "lords" of the land. The Founding Fathers of the newest nation in the world believed that keeping the rewards (the harvests or the profits) from one's own property was a God-given right, and that the nation as a whole would benefit from the prosperity of each individual. Therefore, under the republican system of Christian-inspired government, capitalism thrived, and the United States of America became the wealthiest and strongest nation in the world. Self-authorized bureaucratic gluttony, excessive taxation, unchecked government growth and regulation, uncontrolled spending and accumulation of debt, dangerous foreign alliances, and the excising of religious principles from government activity—all things warned against by the Founding Fathers—began to threaten that system late in the 20th century.

More specifically, every federal agency from the Internal Revenue Service to the Environmental Protection Agency to the U.S. Fish and Wildlife Service, by the 1990s, had swollen to overflowing with *thousands* of bureaucratic zealots enforcing *thousands* of self-serving regulations—most of them having the effect of choking off property rights.

Taxation had burgeoned within a few short decades from about ten percent of earned income to as much as 50 percent. Out-of-control big-government spending far exceeded even this massive confiscation of the people's wealth until the richest nation in the world became nearly the largest debtor nation in the world—*affecting the*

The Sanctity of Property

security of all property.

Several consecutive administrations seemed bent on tying all American activities to huge foreign alliances—the Tri-Lateral Commission, the North Atlantic Treaty Organization (NATO), the United Nations, the North American Free Trade Agreement (NAFTA), the World Trade Organization (WTO), and dozens more.

Let us be reminded that on the topic of foreign alliances, George Washington, while encouraging "good faith and justice toward all nations," cautioned against compromising American sovereignty:

> *The great rule of conduct for us, in regard to foreign nations, is . . . to have with them as little political connection as possible . . . It is our true policy to steer clear of permanent alliances with any portion of the foreign world. . . . Against the insidious wiles of foreign influence . . . the jealousy of a free people ought to be* constantly *awake, since history and experience prove that foreign influence is one of the most baneful foes of republican government.*

Further, Thomas Jefferson, in his first Inaugural Address, championed the notion that " . . . *the enjoyment of life, liberty, property, and peace* . . . " was attainable while exercising " . . . *honest friendship with all nations, entangling alliances with none.*"

Unmindful of the painstaking care and wisdom with which the Founders fashioned their unique democratic (free) republic, modern political leaders, believing themselves to be more enlightened and knowledgeable than their predecessors, "entangled" the U.S. in international alliances that would have controls over birth rates, commerce, the monetary system, the environment and natural resources, private property and much more.

The sanctity of property was lost.

Government had taken a different stand with respect to private property. Department of the Interior Secretary Bruce Babbitt, with the full blessing of President Bill Clinton, advocated sacrificing the "individualistic view of property" in favor of a more "communitarian interpretation." Removing the veil of diplomatic euphemisms, Babbitt's vision included removing fences and all private rights to property. Contrary to the limited constitutional authority allowing the federal government to own land only for placement of the nation's capitol (ten square miles), as well as " . . . *the Erection of Forts, Magazines, Arsenals, dock-Yards, and other needful Buildings . . . "*, by 1990, various agencies within the government were actively acquiring private property from the nation's landowners at the rate of 1,000 acres per day. Millions more acres of private land had become useless to owners through government "management" of wetlands, endangered species, wild and scenic rivers, national parks, and other anti-property "programs."

Governor Fife Symington of Arizona, where a hard-fought battle over property rights occurred in 1994, believed the importance of private property had not changed:

> *To say that property is the cornerstone of liberty comes up short. I would say that property is liberty. . . . You start fooling around with private property rights and you are on the road to slavery. The only thing left with any power at all would be a large central government.*

In 1858, Abraham Lincoln wrote of an inclusive key element necessary to the preservation of liberty:

> *What constitutes the bulwark of our own liberty and independence? It is not our frowning battlements, our bristling sea coasts, the guns of our war steamers, or the strength of our gallant and disciplined army. These are not our reliance against a resumption of tyranny in our fair land. All of them may be turned against our liberties, without making us stronger or weaker for the struggle. Our reliance is in the* love of liberty *which God has planted in our bosoms. Our defense is in the preservation of the spirit which prizes liberty as the heritage of all men, in all lands, everywhere. Destroy this spirit, and you have planted the seeds of despotism around your own doors.*

Two hundred years after the founding of America, the "seeds of despotism" had been cast wide by corrupt forces within a changed Federal Government.

The designers of the Great American Experiment believed the three fundamental principles of free republican government were the rights of personal security, liberty and *private property*. They were God-given individual rights. Government was meant only to *secure* them. Abraham Lincoln saw the *love* of God-given liberty as its only means of defense.

By the second half of the 20th century, the " . . . *spirit which prizes liberty as the heritage of all men* . . . " had long been absent from a federal government that practiced condemnation of private property in order to possess it, that rendered private land useless in deference to endangered rats, that even imprisoned landowners for *improving* worthless so-called "wetlands."

So what went wrong with the Founders' impeccable vision?

It was corrupted by mortal men inserting themselves into the role of God as new self-empowered givers of rights. They began to believe that from powerful government positions they could, and *would*, decide what was in the best interests of citizens, thereby furthering the best interests of themselves. They became the thieves of private property, of personal liberties—of "unalienable" rights granted by God.

In 1513, Italian statesman Machiavelli explained the rationale:

> *Pretexts for taking away the property are never wanting; for he who has once begun to live by robbery will always find pretexts for seizing what belongs to others.*

The U.S. Government has found many "pretexts" for taking away private property. Daniel Webster, in 1820, considered one of them—the element of greed, which knows no distinction between bandits and bureaucrats:

> *In the nature of things, those who have no property and see their neighbors possess much more than they think them to need, cannot be favorable to laws made for the protection of property. When this class becomes numerous, it grows clamorous. It looks on property as its prey and plunder, and is naturally ready, at time, for violence and revolution.*

In the tone of a true patriot, Arizona's Governor Symington summarized the contribution of private property to the success of the American Dream:

> *For anyone who doubts the importance or the power of private property, two things ought to be prescribed. First, take a look around the world during the closing decades of this 20th century. The crumbling Communist Bloc reduced to its most basic meaning is one grand affirmation of the power of private property. And second, just take a look around you here at home. Consider the greatness of this nation and its historical gift for generating capital and wealth. There has never been anything like it in the history of mankind. And from the beginning, these things have been built*

entirely on a foundation of private property rights. It's just that simple. That's where it begins and that's where it ends. That's the cradle of freedom.

That "cradle of freedom" was part of a new unique and nearly perfect system of government born only because its framers embraced the superior wisdom and guidance of God. Legislative, Judicial and Executive usurpations of that wisdom and guidance have reduced the American Experiment to an unstable and fragmented process. To shore it up again, the sanctity of private property must be reasserted as akin to godliness.

. . . a just estimate of the happiness of our country will never overlook what belongs to the fertile activity of a free people, and the benign influence of a responsible government.

James Madison

*Where there is a necessity of the military power .
. . a wise and prudent People will always have a
watchful and a jealous eye over it; for the maxims
and rules of the army are essentially different from
the genius of a free people, and the laws of a free
government.*

Samuel Adams

Chapter Seven:

Nothing New

As important as private property in the scheme of government based on Creator-endowed liberties was the ability to defend and preserve the experiment. It is essential to note here that the Second Amendment to the Constitution was not devised as a protection for the possession of sporting weapons, nor was it originally intended as a provision for individual self-defense. Fortunately, weapons used for gathering meat and warding off criminals are also effective for discouraging governmental tyranny. The Founding Fathers carried fresh recollections of the repugnant nature of King George III's despotic rule, and they designed the simplest of the ten amendments comprising the Bill of Rights to forever prevent a recurrence.

The fight between good and evil is as old as history itself. Philosophies of socialism, communism, Marxism, and other forms of aggressive, dictatorial government, are nothing new. The greatest civilizations throughout recorded history have crumbled from within, destroyed by epidemic corruption, excessive taxation, and moral and social decay. Oppression and tyranny have always come from government, and desires for liberty and freedom have always originated from the masses. This is nothing new, and those who refuse to learn from the pages of history are doomed to repeat it.

Indeed, it was governmental tyranny and oppression which drove the Founders toward the making of America—a new nation based on God's law and " . . . *dedicated to the proposition that all men are created equal* . . . " During 200 years of successful republican government in America, there has occurred a gradual evolution toward the philosophies of Marxist socialism—the same philosophies responsible for enslaving and subjugating millions in the past. Americans are hearing the knock of tyranny at their doors. The thresholds of liberty are giving way. This is nothing new!

The words of a 20th century world leader reflect the trends of the time:

> *This year will go down in history . . . For the first time, a civilized nation has full gun registration! Our streets will be safer, our police more efficient, and the world will follow our lead into the future.*

Does this statement sound familiar? Reviews of nightly newscasts or video coverage on C-SPAN might suggest Charles Shumer, Diane Feinstein, Howard Metzenbaum, Al Gore or Bill Clinton as the author of this "civilized" view on gun control. While its source has been disputed by some experts, others have given credit for this particular quotation to Adolf Hitler.

Gun and other arms control is nothing new either. Before guns existed governments attempted to confiscate swords, bows and arrows, cimeters, axes and knives. Edicts of this nature invariably led to mass murders, subjugations and acts of genocide. Many attempts by governments to disarm, to register, to confiscate guns, have been etched indelibly into our histories. And yet, *not one* specific incident of gun control, gun registration or any confiscation of weapons can be credited with saving lives, protecting citizens, decreasing violence, creating peace, or securing the principles of liberty.

Wake up, America! Has history not taught us a thing?

In the brief span of its 200-year existence, the United States of America has become recognized as the greatest country in the world. The reason? Freedom. The blueprint for freedom has been our inspired Constitution, designed to protect God-given rights. The vision and knowledge of the Founders should serve as timeless lessons for continued success of the American Experiment.

Richard Henry Lee, in 1787, said, "To preserve liberty, it is essential that the whole body of the people always possess arms . . . " Why, then, would Shumer, Feinstein, Metzenbaum, Gore and Clinton, along with other politicians, mayors, commissioners, police officials and organized anti-gun groups, support the disarming of America—an effective death sentence imposed on the tenets of liberty? Such action in 1776 would have been considered treasonous. In contemporary times, cries of treason have given way to socialistic demands for mainstream "political correctness."

Other Founding Fathers defined and defended the eternal principles of liberty. Patrick Henry, while trying to motivate his fellow countrymen to action in 1775, spoke of limitations on freedom:

> *They tell us that we are weak—unable to cope with so formidable an adversary. But when shall we be stronger? Will it be next week or next year? Will it be when we are totally disarmed, and when a guard will be stationed in every house?*

Does this not sound like a description of President Clinton's 1994 crime bill, which calls for banning weapons of defense and assigning as many as 100,000 additional police officers into private neighborhoods? This is not new. England's King George III did it, too. Colonists fought the Revolutionary War over similar tyrannical oppression.

Thomas Jefferson addressed the issue of gun control in 1764:

> *Laws that forbid the carrying of arms serve rather to encourage than to prevent homicides, for an unarmed man may be attacked with greater confidence than an armed man. Laws that forbid the carrying of arms . . . disarm only those who are neither inclined nor determined to commit crimes . . . Such laws make things worse for the assaulted and better for the assailants.*

The Second Amendment did not *give* the right to keep and bear arms; the right came from Almighty God. Self-protection is an unalienable right with which we were endowed by our Creator. It is nothing new. The Second Amendment is a limitation to and a direct order for government to obey. Federal employees and public servants have a sworn duty to obey the Bill of Rights just as a soldier has a sworn obligation to respect the orders of his general. Imagine the chaos resulting from a soldier summarily refusing to obey an officer's command until he obtains an interpretation from the Supreme Court!

We, the people of the Republic of the United States of America, are the generals in charge of securing compliance with constitutional orders as established by the Founding Fathers. Insubordination, government criminality, treason and usurpation of power cannot be tolerated. To allow these actions is to undermine the U.S. Constitution. Further, to undermine the Constitution is to threaten liberty and the very existence of America.

Attempts to do so are nothing new!

We can safely rely on the disposition of the state legislatures to erect barriers against the encroachment of the national authority.

James Madison

Chapter Eight:

Godless World Government

The Founding Fathers and their ideals for Christian-based republican government have been sold out by a succession of contemporary American presidents. For decades, U.S. leadership in Washington has pledged total allegiance to the United Nations and a so-called United Nations Peace Force. In 1961, the State Department adopted "The United States Program for General and Complete Disarmament in a Peaceful World." Disarmament goals and objectives are listed in the program summary:

111

The over-all goal of the United States is a free, secure, and peaceful world of independent states adhering to common standards of justice and international conduct and subjecting the use of force to the rule of law; a world which has achieved general and complete disarmament under effective international control; and a world in which adjustment to change takes place in accordance with the principles of the United Nations.

Under this program the United Nations would police the world, and there would exist no higher authority for appeal. Any attempt to resist the organization would be considered "adjustment to change," and dealt with strictly in accordance with U.N. "principles"—whatever those may be.

American sovereignty does not exist under this plan, and God is no part of it. The United Nations becomes the almighty " . . . *institution of effective means for the enforcement of international agreements, for the settlement of disputes, and for the maintenance of peace . . .* " The State Department document further supports the " . . . *establishment and effective operation of an International Disarmament Organization within the framework of the United Nations to insure compliance at all times . . .* "

This does not allow for exceptions. U.S. military superiority in the world would become diluted to the status of an internal police force, and the citizens of the heretofore strongest and freest nation in the world would be "protected" by armies made up of soldiers from foreign lands.

Cleverly, though, American autocrats devised a method for maintaining dictatorial control over American citizens. Dozens of Executive Orders dealing with the occurrence of a "national emergency" have been quietly signed by presidents dating back to Franklin D. Roosevelt. Any declaration of a national emergency causes all of them to become effective.

On May 30, 1992, President George Bush executed his signature on Executive Order 12808. The document defined a ". . . *declared national emergency to deal with the unrest and extraordinary threat to national security, foreign policy and economy of the United States constituted by policies of the governments of Serbia and Montenegro.*" EO 12808, as published in the *Federal Register*, was meant to have a life span of one year. To keep it alive, President Clinton signed a "Notice of Extension" on May 27, 1993.

Chords of incredulity rang loudly over any "threat to national security" brought by a civil war within Bosnia. The U.S. had virtually no interest, economic or otherwise, in this tiny Eastern nation. However, there were other reasons to keep the U.S. tied to what Thomas Jefferson called "entangling alliances" with remote nations of the world. An unpublicized state of emergency precipitated by internal war in some obscure region of the world was enough to enhance a demonic plan for total domestic control and eventual governmental allegiance with the "New World Order"— one-world government.

To further ensure the process, Bush, before leaving office, also signed Executive Orders 12810 and

12831—each dealing with aspects of the same "crisis." Clinton subsequently signed EO 12846, on the same subject.

Why was the war between Muslims, Serbs and Croats in faraway Bosnia so critically important to the national security of the United States? Nothing could be more absurd. In reality it only provided the "excuse" needed for a tyrannical American president to retain the option of declaring martial law over the people of his *own country* if he should so choose.

There are dozens of Executive Orders published in the *Federal Register* that automatically come into play in the event of a "national emergency." Orders published numerically from 10995 through 11005 allow for federal takeover of media communications, electrical power and other fuels, food resources, infrastructure and transportation, citizen work forces, health care systems, cities, railroads and waterways. Order 11490 takes control of personal banking accounts.

There are more—many more. Ideally, they might have been written to apply to a real national emergency within the borders of the U.S., but technically they provide dictatorial power to the President during the time of any declared national emergency—hence, the need for Bush's EO 12808 and Clinton's extension of it. Ambitious and corrupt political leaders worry about the castrating effects of having no "national emergency" to empower them beyond the limitations of the Constitution.

As a sign of commitment to the New World Order, Bill Clinton signed Presidential Decision Directive 25 on May 5, 1993, effectively placing U.S. military officers under

United Nations' command. The document was originally written as Presidential Review Directive 13, containing Joint Chiefs of Staff Chairman General Colin Powell's insistence that " . . . *U.S. commanders under UN command . . . not comply with orders which they·believe are: (1) outside the mandate of the mission, (2) illegal under U.S. law, or, (3) militarily imprudent or unsound.*" Bill Clinton removed Powell's language after the general retired. The revised document became PDD-25.

The United Nations is the axis around which efforts to establish a one-world government revolve. In 1990, a ten-year series of world summit conferences was planned on "pressing development issues." The first held was the 1990 World Summit for Children, in New York, at which UN intervention into the traditional family unit was advocated. The 1992 Earth Summit in Rio de Janeiro produced a "biodiversity treaty" which, in effect, would surrender control and management of the world's resources and ecosystems to the UN. In 1993, an international conference on human rights, conducted in Vienna, suggested world population control might best be managed by the UN. At the March 1995 World Summit for Social Development, the leaders of more than 100 obscure Third World nations offered up plans for "social development" within their own nations, all with demanding hands out toward America. Other topics for planned conferences included women's issues and a "city summit."

If the United Nations was founded for the honorable and noble mission of promoting peace around the world, then why has it become engaged in efforts to separate and control families? What is the good in a plan to register children with identifying numbers? What business of the UN are ecosystems and resources in America? Where is the logic behind a conference on "human rights" in 1993 followed by a conference on population control (genocide?) in 1994?

What exactly is the "New World Order?"

President Bush coined its name, and Bill Clinton began clearly defining it by committing U.S. troops like expendable mercenaries to all sorts of foreign bloodbaths under U.N. authority. The national interests were never threatened by civil wars in Somalia, Rwanda or Bosnia, but U.S. troops were there and American lives were lost on every "peacekeeping" front. When Somalians murdered an American soldier, then dragged his body for hours through the streets, Clinton decried the outrage of it all but did nothing to retaliate. To do so would have been to hinder progress toward a one-world government.

Under Clinton's plan to become a powerful figure within the New World Order, millions of American tax dollars were spent to juggle dictators in Haiti. At the same time, America's fighting forces were reduced to the level of a pitiful "peace corps." Clinton asked permission of United Nations bureaucrats to involve U.S. forces in Haiti and other world locations, but he did not ask the approval of Congress, as required by the Constitution. He signed PDD-25, which specifically asserts his authority " . . . *to place U.S. forces under the operational control of a foreign commander.*"

Embracing the plan for one-world government,

Clinton supported world trade agreements like the General Agreement on Tariffs and Trade (GATT) and the North American Free Trade Agreement (NAFTA). He fought for alliance within the World Trade Organization (WTO), which effectively placed American jobs, trade and the economy under control of a foreign legislature within which the U.S. has only one of 123 votes—most of them from Third World nations. The once-envied bargaining power of the U.S. was left even more impotent by a foreign trade tribunal empowered to settle disputes within the WTO— unconditionally and *in secret!*

Bill Clinton, in his quest for world unity, has supported and fought for ratification of nightmarish international treaties because, by their very nature, they supersede U.S. federal law and even the protections of the U.S. Constitution. Some examples include the Law of the Sea Treaty, an international noose around the neck of American superiority, committing Western wealth and technology to Third World nations; the United Nations Treaty on the Rights of the Child, a reckless plan to transfer the traditional rights of parents concerning the rearing, discipline, education, health and welfare of their children, all to a new international bureaucracy; the United Nations Treaty on Discrimination Against Women, an effort to place the traditional rights of American women in the hands of a committee of foreign "experts" who would make binding decisions about child care, abortion, comparable worth and even "interpersonal relationships."

Striving to be more than a little duck in a very large pond, Bill Clinton surrounded himself in the Office of

President with Marxist socialists like Strobe Talbot, a lifelong advocate of one-world government who has long believed in abolishing the "obsolete" notions of nationhood and national sovereignty.

What is missing from this plan?

God!

Third World dictatorships do not know God. Warring tribes in distant lands do not know God. The United Nations does not know God. Bill Clinton, Al Gore, Strobe Talbot, Bruce Babbitt, and so many more single-sighted politicians and bureaucrats, worship *another* god— Power. In order to establish a one-world government—the "New World Order"—God must be kept from the process. That means the inspired documents and philosophies upon which the American Experiment in republican self-government was founded must be rendered obsolete, antiquated—nonexistent. The Declaration of Independence must be made to seem like the folly of a few radical colonists. The U.S. Constitution must be "interpreted" to the point of ineffectiveness. The Bill of Rights must be abandoned. After all, protections afforded the early colonists surely were not meant to apply to later (wiser) generations. The teaching of religion and government— even quotations by the Founding Fathers—must be removed from classrooms. The American system of government must be dismantled from the foundation up. The way to do that is to break down its supports—God-given unalienable rights.

The right to life (personal security) is diminished by government restrictions on guns in the hands of law-abiding citizens while social entitlements encourage the epidemic spread of capital crime. The right to personal liberty is stripped away by creating a nation of subjects dependent on government welfare, health care, employment benefits, food and other handouts. The pursuit of happiness is stifled by federal agencies bent on destroying the American system of free enterprise by shutting down industries in deference to animals, by regulating private property out of production, by excessive taxation and regulation, by controlling land, water, money, industry, and by creating more and bigger bureaucracies whose mission it is to "manage" all aspects of citizens' lives.

A nation of serfs will not resist the New World Order. That's why the political agenda of Bill Clinton included removing guns from the hands of the people, registering every American in a socialistic health care system, strangling household budgets with punitive taxes, and flinging billions of dollars around the world in futile foreign aid schemes while signing international treaties designed to erode American sovereignty.

Bill Clinton is a Marxist. He believes in godless socialism. Creator-endowed unalienable rights provided Clinton with little more than aggravation as they stood in the way of his grand plan. Only after American voters changed the 40-year-old face of party leadership in Washington on November 8, 1994, did Clinton make overtures toward an angry public suggesting he might become more conservative. Some gullible Americans bought it. The President's popularity rating improved. In reality, Clinton realized achieving the New World Order was impossible in the two years remaining in his first term. Therefore, he must win again in 1996 to accomplish his dream before the year 2000.

For most of the 20th century destructive chisels chipped away at the inspired Constitution and Bill of Rights. The driving hammers were wielded by Congress and the courts. The Federal Government ballooned to enormous proportions, its self-empowered bureaucracies functioning as arbitrary, unchallenged legislatures. The states and the citizens became subjects to a government they had learned to perceive as the most powerful entity in the world. Individual sovereignty became meaningless to federal-level officials.

A resounding cry of resistance was heard from the American people on November 8, 1994. It was a cry that severely curtailed Bill Clinton's covert plan, because it was a cry that said individual sovereignty had *not* become meaningless to the people of the nation. The final alignment of America with the New World Order will come only when individual sovereignty has been surrendered—when the *people* are irreversibly dependent upon the federal government for *everything*.

Bill Clinton entered the Presidency convinced he would leave his mark in the history books as the American president who led the nation into allegiance with godless one-world government. He would not abandon his plan for the will of the people or the good of the nation. Clinton (or his successors) will be rendered incapable of executing the plan only by patriotic Americans willing to rise up in defense of the U.S. Constitution, armed with unshakable conviction in the principles of freedom as granted by the Creator.

American sovereignty has and will always rest in the hands of those who believe liberty cannot exist outside the presence of God.

. . . there have always been those who wish to enlarge the powers of the General Government. There is but one safe rule . . . confine [it] *within the sphere of its appropriate duties . . . enumerated in the Constitution. . . . Every attempt to exercise power beyond these limits should be promptly and firmly opposed.*

Andrew Jackson

Chapter Nine:

The Proper Role

With regard to the Constitution and the leaders of federal government, Thomas Jefferson said, "It was intended to lace them up straitly within the enumerated powers." The Bill of Rights was then added as an extra measure of protection against government tyranny.

Article I, Section 8 of the U.S. Constitution grants the "general" government of the United States authority only to do certain things, and nothing more:

> . . . *To lay and collect Taxes, Duties, Imposts and Excises, to pay the Debts and provide for the common Defence and general Welfare of the United States;*

To borrow money on the credit of the United States;

To regulate Commerce with foreign Nations, and among the several States, and with the Indian tribes;

To establish an uniform Rule of Naturalization, and uniform Laws on the subject of Bankruptcies throughout the United States;

To coin Money, regulate the value thereof, and of foreign Coin, and fix the Standard of Weights and Measures;

To provide for the Punishment of counterfeiting the Securities and current Coin of the United States;

To establish Post Offices and post Roads;

To promote the Progress of Science and useful Arts, by securing for limited Times to Authors and Inventors the exclusive Right to their respective Writings and Discoveries;

To constitute Tribunals inferior to the Supreme Court;

To define and punish Piracies and Felonies committed on the high Seas, and Offenses against the Law of Nations;

To declare War, grant Letters of Marque and Reprisal, and make Rules concerning Captures on Land and Water;

To raise and support Armies, but no Appropriation of Money to that Use shall be for a longer Time than two Years;

124

To provide and maintain a Navy;

To make Rules for the Government and Regulation of the land and naval Forces;

To provide for calling forth the Militia to execute the Laws of the Union, suppress Insurrections and repel Invasions;

To provide for organizing, arming, and disciplining the Militia, and for governing such Part of them as may be employed in the Service of the United States, reserving to the States respectively, the Appointment of the Officers, and the Authority of training the Militia according to the discipline prescribed by Congress;

To exercise exclusive Legislation in all Cases whatsoever, over such District (not exceeding ten Miles square) as may, by Cession of particular States, and the acceptance of Congress, become the Seat of the Government of the United States, and to exercise like Authority over all Places purchased by the Consent of the Legislature of the State in which the Same shall be, for the Erection of Forts, Magazines, Arsenals, dock-Yards, and other needful Buildings;—And

To make all Laws which shall be necessary and proper for carrying into Execution the foregoing Powers, and all other Powers vested by this Constitution in the Government of the United States, or in any Department or Officer thereof.

The Bill of Rights, then, spelled out specific

restrictions that would prevent the Federal Government from expanding outside these authorized areas:

Amendment I: Congress shall make no law respecting an establishment of religion, or prohibiting the free exercise thereof; or abridging the freedom of speech, or of the press; or the right of the people to peaceably assemble, and to petition the Government for a redress of grievances.

Amendment II: A well regulated Militia, being necessary to the security of a free State, the right of the people to keep and bear arms shall not be infringed.

Amendment III: No Soldier shall, in time of peace be quartered in any house, without consent of the Owner, nor in time of war, but in a manner to be prescribed by law.

Amendment IV: The right of the people to be secure in their persons, houses, papers, and effects, against unreasonable searches and seizures, shall not be violated, and no Warrants shall issue, but upon probable cause, supported by Oath or affirmation, and particularly describing the place to be searched, and the persons or things to be seized.

Amendment V: No person shall be held to answer

for a capital, or otherwise infamous crime, unless on a presentment or indictment of a Grand Jury, except in cases arising in the land and naval forces, or in the Militia, when in actual service in time of War or public danger; nor shall any person be subject for the same offence twice put in jeopardy of life or limb; nor shall be compelled in any criminal case to be a witness against himself, nor be deprived of life, liberty, or property, without due process of law; nor shall private property be taken for public use without just compensation.

Amendment VI: In all criminal prosecutions, the accused shall enjoy the right to a speedy and public trial, by an impartial jury of the State and district wherein the crime shall have been committed, which district shall have been previously ascertained by law, and to be informed of the nature and cause of the accusation; to be confronted with the witnesses against him; to have compulsory process for obtaining witnesses in his favor, and to have the Assistance of Counsel for his defence.

Amendment VII: In Suits at common law, where the value in controversy shall exceed twenty dollars, the right of trial by jury shall be preserved, and no fact tried by a jury, shall be otherwise re-examined in any Court of the United States, than according to the rules of the common law.

> *Amendment VIII: Excessive bail shall not be required, nor excessive fines imposed, nor cruel and unusual punishment inflicted.*

> *Amendment IX: The enumeration of the Constitution, of certain rights, shall not be construed to deny or disparage others retained by the people.*

> *Amendment X: The powers not delegated to the United States by the Constitution, nor prohibited by it to the States, are reserved to the States respectively, or to the people.*

The Enumerated Powers and the Bill of Rights define the authority of the United States Government. There are no exceptions. Any law or rule or regulation imposed beyond these limitations is a usurpation of power. Any legislator, bureaucrat or other government official responsible for making, passing, imposing or enforcing any law or rule or regulation outside these limitations is in violation of the Constitution and guilty of treason. Any gun control law that effectively infringes the right of a law-abiding citizen to keep and bear arms is in conflict with the Constitution, and those responsible for its existence and enforcement are guilty of treason. Any "taking" of private property without just compensation is in conflict with the Constitution, and agents of the government imposing and enforcing the actions are guilty of treason. Taxes imposed for reasons outside Article I, Section 8, are illegal. Again, there are no exceptions.

Thousands—even millions—of governmental abuses of power have occurred throughout the 20th century. They came as the result of a government growing fat on the wealth of a nation, and the people becoming comfortable about a government that seemed capable and willing to take care of everybody. Agencies were created and given rule-making authority that could not be challenged. Legislators became jaded and spoiled, influenced by wealthy special interests. Supreme Court appointees became political pawns with strong party ties. No one seemed to notice the diminishing role of states' rights and local governments. Everyone began to perceive the Federal Government as the most powerful entity in the world. And government itself began to believe it was true.

Thomas Jefferson, James Madison and others among the Founders made it expressly clear in their writings and addresses that their intentions were to throttle the actions of the general government to prevent a recurrence of the kinds of tyranny experienced under the monarchy of King George III. A federal government authorizing power to itself that is forbidden by the Constitution is an act of tyranny of the exact nature feared by the authors of the Constitution.

Ezra Taft Benson defined the proper role of government, as relating to domestic affairs, in three basic principles:

> *. . . that governments were instituted of God for the benefit of man; and that He holds men accountable for their acts in relation to them;*

> *. . . that no government can exist in peace, except such laws are framed and held inviolate as will secure to each individual the free exercise of conscience, the right and control of property, and the protection of life;* [and]
>
> *. . . that all men are bound to sustain and uphold the respective governments in which they reside, while protected in their inherent and inalienable rights by the laws of such governments.*

In summary, Benson said, "In other words, the most important single function of government is to secure the rights and freedoms of individual citizens."

The United States Republic is fundamentally based on the principle that the people are the most powerful authority within the government. Political representatives are elected to represent the people only within the constitutional boundaries pursuant to their oaths of office. Just as public servants are in place to *serve* and *protect* the will of the people, they are also there to *oppose* it if the will of the people becomes evil or in some way unconstitutional.

For example, if a county sheriff arrests an individual for allegedly committing murder, then that sheriff has a constitutional obligation to protect and defend the suspect's rights to due process and a fair trial—even if every other citizen of the county wants to hang the suspect from a tree. "Mobocracy" cannot be allowed in government any more than anarchy or tyranny. The "will of the people" must not be construed as justification to violate the God-given rights of other citizens.

Further, if government derives its power from the people, it follows logically (and lawfully) that the people cannot bestow power they themselves do not have; therefore, government cannot do that which the people cannot lawfully or morally do. If it is illegal, then, for one citizen to take money from another for the purpose of aiding a poverty-stricken neighbor, it is equally illegal for government to engage in the same practice.

The United States Government has no constitutional authority to take away the money or personal property of free citizens for redistribution through social welfare programs. Not even good intentions or critical need are reasons enough to allow government the power to redistribute the wealth of a nation. Private citizens functioning within a system of free enterprise should decide how to use their money. Charity and generosity are virtues of the individual conscience, not of government mandate.

The Founding Fathers' "republic" has evolved steadily toward a socialist state during the 20th century. "Big Brother" has set up hundreds of social programs aimed at caring for the poor and sick, the elderly and handicapped, addicts and criminals. Congress has moved outside the confines of the Constitution to enact most of them. In any such instance, their actions have been illegal. Only the states (the people) can authorize federal action outside the limits of Article I, Section 8, by way of a constitutional amendment. "Feel good" social programs should never have been supported at the high price of freedom and personal choice.

During a large portion of the 20th century, however,

the Federal Government of the United States spent a good deal of energy on denying and stripping away the rights and freedoms of individual citizens. The reasons were many and varied—protection of endangered species, preserving so-called "wetlands" and other environmental causes, burgeoning demand for tax revenues, failed social programs, escalating crime rates, and increased efforts by Marxist liberals to socialize the nation.

Thomas Jefferson believed the formula for successful republican government involved confining the various levels strictly within their own jurisdictions:

> *Let the national government be entrusted with the defence of the nation, and its foreign and federal relations; the State governments with the civil rights, law, police, and administration of what concerns the State generally, the counties with the local concerns of the counties, and each ward direct the interests within itself. It is by dividing and subdividing these republics from the great national one down through all its subordinations . . . that all will be done best.*

The Founding Fathers knew and feared the aspect of human nature that causes greed and gluttony; they believed unrestricted federal authority would result in a return to unrighteous dominion over the masses. Jefferson mused appropriately:

> *What has destroyed liberty and the rights of man in every government which has ever existed under the sun? The generalizing and concentrating all cares and powers into one body.*

The God-given liberties of American citizens have been abused and denigrated commonly in two ways—each one in direct conflict with the limitations and protections of the Constitution.

One, Congress has authorized new federal agencies and bureaucracies, empowering them to do as they see fit in the performance of their respective "duties," until we have become a nation of subjects controlled by a government of unaccountable powercrats. These federal agencies (U.S. Fish and Wildlife Service, the Environmental Protection Agency, etc.) are unconstitutional because they concentrate all the functions of the legislative, judicial and executive branches under one agency head or cabinet secretary. They have the power to make rules, to enforce them and adjudicate penalties.

Second, the Supreme Court—having empowered itself in 1806 as the last authority in constitutional issues—evolved during the last half of the 20th century as the Supreme Legislature. In a capacity superior to any appeal, the Court became the most powerful voice in the nation on the issues of capital punishment, prayer in schools, pornography, abortion, the "rights" of criminals, private property, and many other areas regarding the quality of life among "free" Americans. In direct conflict with constitutional guarantees, the Court established precedents of restricting the power of states and cities, even neutralizing state laws and local ordinances that had been passed by large majorities of voting citizens.

Government outside the bounds of the Constitution is tyranny. That is why the Founders relied so consistently on Christian principles for direction. In recognizing the importance of the influence of God, the inspired authors of the founding documents proclaimed His authority as their basis of law—*natural* law. The Founders were convinced that laws, liberties and rights were the gifts of God, and the Constitution was written as a vehicle to apply those elements to the Great American Experiment.

At the conclusion of their great work, James Madison acknowledged the presence of divine influence in *The Federalist*, No. 37:

> *It is impossible for the man of pious reflection not to perceive in it a finger of that Almighty hand which has been so frequently and signally extended to our relief in the critical stage of revolution.*

The Declaration of Independence, the U.S. Constitution and the Bill of Rights leave no doubt as to the proper role of government. Few contemporary political leaders, however, have read even one of these "documents of freedom" from beginning to end. They govern without the knowledge of what our government was meant to be, and what made it successful from the outset. Fewer than those who have read the inspired documents are those who object to the removal of God from the republican process. Again, government outside the bounds of the Constitution is tyranny.

      Freedom outside the influence of God is futile.

A multitude of laws in a country is like a great number of physicians, a sign of weakness and malady.

François Marie de Voltaire

II:

Religious Perspective

We say that the Constitution of the United States is a glorious standard; it is founded in the wisdom of God.

Joseph Smith

Chapter Ten:

By a Single Thread

In our portrayal
of God as the indispensable bridge between liberty and government, I wanted to share a personal story. My friend and co-author Tim Walters agreed to indulge me.

After filing a lawsuit against the Federal Government over the Brady Handgun Control Act in 1994, I met with a great deal of notoriety and media attention. I never understood why. I simply refused to be enlisted through federal legislation into working for the Federal Government—as mandated by the Brady Act—when my constitutional obligation lay in serving as the elected sheriff of Graham County, Arizona. I had no idea that taking my oath of office seriously would become so newsworthy.

Naturally, I had a variety of experiences with the media—articles reflecting views contrary to what I had said or who I am, and some portrayals of me that were entirely untrue. On the other hand, I made some enduring friendships with reporters truly dedicated to their craft and committed to their God-given freedom of press.

One such reporter came to me from the *Dallas Morning News*. Her name was Terry. We spent the day together, visiting my family and associates. Back at my office at the end of the day, Terry said, "May I ask you a personal question?"

I assured her she could ask me anything.

She turned a page in her note pad, then asked, "Does your religion have anything to do with what you have done —standing against the Brady Bill?"

Terry was the only reporter who had ever asked me that question. I thought her query was insightful, yet not too surprising following her visits to my home and that of my parents. Initially, I was uneasy about answering her question —not that I was embarrassed or ashamed, just nervous that she might use my response to color me as a fanatical Mormon in love with guns. Nevertheless, the question was legitimate, and Terry seemed sincere.

I told her the truth. "Yes, it does." After a moment, I added, "As long as I can remember I've been taught that freedom is something worth fighting and dying for—and that the Constitution was inspired by God."

Terry left it at that; she made no further inquiries.

Later, I found myself reflecting on my own answer. I realized then how much I had learned at a very young age about the Constitution and the value of freedom during my upbringing in the Mormon church.

One of my earliest recollections about the Constitution was a prophecy from the president and latter-day founder of the Mormon church, Joseph Smith:

> *The time will come when the constitution of this nation will hang, as it were, by a single thread.*

Every member of the Mormon faith has been charged with the duty and responsibility to restore and save the Constitution from utter destruction. Basic Mormon theology teaches:

(1) freedom is a gift of Almighty God;

(2) vigilance, hard work, the courage to fight for what is right, and faith in God are essential in preserving liberty;

(3) the Constitution was divinely inspired, formulated by men whom God had raised up for that purpose; and,

(4) the kingdom of God cannot survive the destruction of eternal principles of justice and free agency.

Why do these Mormon tenets sound so familiar? It's almost as if Thomas Jefferson or Benjamin Franklin had a hand in their creation.

Many leaders of the Church of Jesus Christ of Latter-day Saints have issued strong warnings and prophecies relating to freedom and God's law. Church President David O. McKay allowed for no condition or compromise:

> *Next to being one in worshiping God, there is nothing in this world upon which this church should be more united than upholding and defending the Constitution of the United States. I refer to the fundamental principle of the gospel—free agency. References in the scriptures show that this principle is essential to man's salvation . . .*

L.D.S. President John Taylor reiterated:

> *When the people shall have torn to shreds the Constitution of the United States, the elders of Israel will be found holding it up to the nations of earth proclaiming liberty.*

Is there yet a great many years before the Constitution will hang by a thread? Or can Americans take comfort in believing "this is still a free country?"

I think not.

Americans today find most aspects of their daily lives controlled, mandated, licensed, inspected, permitted, or monitored in some way by a myriad of government bureaucracies. The food we eat is checked and regulated by the Food and Drug Administration, then taxed at the point of purchase. To operate our privately-owned vehicles requires compliance with many government mandates from speed restrictions to licensing, from registration

142

requirements to emissions testing. Our homes must be built by licensed contractors within government-approved zones according to certain fixed standards. We pay taxes on our property and comply with government restrictions on when we may or may not light fires in our fireplaces.

Farmers are forced to plow and plant according to government deadlines. Ranchers jump through impossible hoops relative to grazing fees, water rights, access, improvements and environmental protection. Teachers and lawyers, accountants and cops, judges, doctors, all must be government certified and licensed. Recreationists cannot hunt or fish, camp or hike, shoot or even pick flowers in the forest without government permits.

We are forced by government to give up our money and personal property to perpetuate social welfare programs. Our tax dollars are squandered on "foreign aid" to corrupt distant governments who never repay their debts. At the same time, American citizens are jailed for failing to "report" capital gains, gratuities, inheritances and gifts.

No facet of our lives is untouched by government regulation. God-given rights were never meant to be controlled by government. James Madison called it "intermeddling." The Constitution did not *give* us liberty; it was created to *protect* the gift of liberty as given by God. Judicial interpretations of this inspired document, however, have served to weaken its effectiveness.

Let's be realistic. Just and caring government is essential to providing for the maintenance of law and order. Without laws there would be anarchy and chaos. Law and order can and should coexist with liberty. Liberty, however, should never be sacrificed to achieve law and order. The Constitution does not need interpretation. It does not need to be fixed or changed; it needs to be *obeyed!*

The U.S. Constitution *is* hanging by a thread. Its shreds are hanging all around us. They are vivid reminders that liberty and wickedness *cannot* coexist.

A Bill of Rights is what the People are entitled to against every Government on Earth . . . and what no just Government should refuse . . .

Thomas Jefferson

The strength of the constitution lies entirely in the determination of each citizen to defend it.

Albert Einstein

Chapter Eleven:

Free Agency

The concept of free agency did not originate with the concept of republican government. Free agency is a fundamental God-given gift. It is a concept that originated with the Creator of all things, and was "endowed" upon mankind as an essential element of "unalienable rights." The rights to life, liberty and property cannot exist without the facilitating ingredient of free agency.

As the moral fiber of America becomes frayed and weak, free agency becomes the victim of governmental action. Socialistic politicians look for superficial remedies to societal problems in expensive entitlement programs that typically aggravate the problems and ultimately fail. Every new social program chokes off free agency a little more than the one before it. Without free agency, liberty is lost and government dominates. Therefore, it's imperative that we understand the correlation between political degradation and spiritual decay.

To comprehend spiritual decay, one must first accept man's spiritual origin and the Master's plan for His children. In Jeremiah 1:5, God makes it expressly clear that humankind existed before physical birth in a premortal life:

> *Before I formed thee in the belly I knew thee; and before thou camest forth out of the womb I sanctified thee, and I ordained thee a prophet unto the nations.*

Such a prior relationship between God and Jeremiah could not have been possible without a spiritual preexistence. Jeremiah is not the only one who experienced it; we all did. During this premortal period we were all introduced to God's plan for His children. We participated in a "war" over philosophies, and we each made a conscious choice to follow one "plan" over another. This is where we first learned about "free agency" and the eternal nature of freedom.

A war in Heaven was waged over the very essence of freedom. Satan offered his plan, and Christ offered His. Thus began the eternal battle of "good versus evil."

Satan came forth amidst the councils of Heaven and proposed that we all follow him. His plan was a simple one with terrific results. He suggested that all God's children be *forced* to live righteously, guaranteeing their salvation and their return to Heaven. The plan only required that we all give up our personal freedom, our right to choose—our free agency.

Jesus, on the other hand, proposed a plan for salvation in which he would offer up himself to atone for man's sins, and allow us to make our own choices—to repent, to learn and to grow, to choose good or evil, and to accept the responsibility and consequences of our choices.

This "War in Heaven" is portrayed effectively in the play *My Turn On Earth*, by Lex de Azevedo and Doug Stewart:

> Satan: *I have a plan.*
> *It will save every man.*
> *I will force them to live righteously.*
> *They won't have to choose;*
> *Not one we will lose,*
> *And give all the glory to me.*
> *This is the way;*
> *Not a thing you will pay.*
> *Any problems and pain will not be.*
> *No wars and no strife,*
> *A wonderful life,*
> *And give all the glory to me.*
> *Free?*
> *Nobody needs to be free!*

Jesus: *I have a plan.*
It is better for man;
Each will have to decide what to be.
In choosing, I know
You'll learn and you'll grow,
And, Father, the glory to Thee.
This is the way;
Each must learn to obey,
And, Father, the glory to thee.
Everyone needs to be free!

In subsequent lines, Satan brands Jesus a "warmonger" and warns against "wars, bloodshed and crime" befalling those who do not follow him. Finally, he promises, "I will see to it personally that all of you are taken care of . . . "

Jesus responds, "I cannot promise you the same." He adds there will be dangers and difficulties, but insists, "You must have the opportunity to choose . . . not to look continually to someone else for guidance . . . we must use our own free agency."

What is the familiar note peeling forth from Satan's plan? Has not the United States Federal Government positioned itself to "take care of us?" In doing so, has it not limited our personal choices, mandated our behavior and negated our responsibility?

Many Americans have been "conditioned" into wickedness and corruption by an unholy government taking care of them. They live in government houses, eat government food, spend government money and wear government clothes. When their subsidies are not enough, they turn to fraud, deception and crime to obtain more. Their abortions are financed by the government, and their crimes are treated with government leniency and rehabilitation programs. They have learned how *not* to work and achieve—how not to *choose.*

"Pro-choice" has become the cry-word for abortion-rights activists during recent decades, but the term is an oxymoron. Those who truly subscribe to the principle of personal choice must also believe in personal accountability and responsibility for the consequences of making choices. Abortion denies *someone* the God-given right to life. The person who makes that "choice" is accountable for that choice. Those who hide behind the constitutional right of privacy to avoid their accountability are guilty of violating God's Law, laws of nature and constitutional intent. It is no accident that government perpetually fires the debates over abortion and other social degeneracy.

The tactics of "Big Brother" government are the tactics of Satan, as described in his "plan." They are designed to rob away God-given rights and freedom. They are clear evidence that the War in Heaven has never ended. After Satan's plan was rejected, he and his followers were cast out. Satan pledged to do all he could to thwart God's plan—to destroy the free agency of man! Free Americans must recognize the dearth of freedom throughout the world for what it is.

Satan has many tools with which to destroy free agency. Hate and greed and bigotry. Violence and crime. Power and corruption. Drug abuse and alcoholism.

Communism, socialism, tyranny. Disobedience of God's laws. God created man to be free, and gifted him with the ability to choose between good and evil. The heavy hand of government makes choosing more difficult when the choices are regulated, licensed, taxed and mandated.

No one can serve two masters. Christians cannot obey God's law and follow Satan's plan, too. It is the God-given responsibility of free Americans to save the inspired U.S. Constitution from destruction by evil forces from without and within. To do so, we must turn away from Satan and shore up our own spiritual foundations. We have the ability, and we have the choice.

It's called "free agency."

I have now disposed of all my property to my family. There is one thing more I wish I could give them, and that is the Christian religion. If they had that, and I had not given them one shilling, they would have been rich, and if they had not that, and I had given them all the world, they would be poor.

Patrick Henry

I believe there are more instances of the abridgement of freedom of the people by gradual and silent encroachments of those in power than by violent and sudden usurpations.

James Madison

Chapter Twelve:

Secret Combinations

Perhaps one of the most glaring examples of godlessness in American government was the murder of John F. Kennedy in 1963. Circumstances surrounding the tragedy, however, were not as America has been led to believe. Only the government claims Kennedy's assassination was the work of a lone gunman.

Throughout history, governments and political organizations leaving dark scars upon the history of humankind have worn many titles. They have been called "secret societies," underground organizations, mafiosos, communists, fascists, Marxists, socialists, and others. *The Book of Mormon* called them "secret combinations." No matter their names, evidence of their existence is irrefutable.

155

It's confusing to note that many popular conservative radio and television talk show hosts, acclaimed in the 1990s as champions of political virtue and common sense, will not say the "c" word—CONSPIRACY. Even Rush Limbaugh, the most revered of them all, has avoided discussing the New World Order. In contrast to this deliberate expurgation, the March 14, 1994, issue of *Time* magazine carried an article entitled "How To Achieve the New World Order," by Henry Kissinger. The former secretary of state argued the U.S. must compromise its idealism with a more "pragmatic approach" in dealing with international relations. The article pointed out, "Both Bill Clinton and George Bush have spoken of the new world order as if it were just around the corner."

Whether American citizens support the idea, damn the concept or deny its existence, the New World Order conspiracy has been upon us for a long time. It's implementation *is* "just around the corner." American involvement in the World Trade Organization, the World Bank, the Council on Foreign Relations, the Tri-Lateral Commission, the World Monetary Fund and the United Nations—to name only a few—is evidence of continued efforts to dissolve the concept of nationhood in favor of one-world government.

Conspiratorial organizations are nothing new; corruption in government is as old as government itself. Secret societies, motivated by greed, hate, power and bigotry, have long controlled governments through financial manipulation, wars, scandals and assassinations. There is strong evidence to suggest that Abraham Lincoln was the victim of such a conspiracy.

More obviously, the assassination of John Kennedy can be shown as the result of a complex conspiracy. National surveys conducted in the late 1960s revealed nearly 80 percent of all Americans believed more than one person was involved in the murder of the president. And yet, most citizens are reluctant to challenge the findings of "official" investigative commissions. They *want* to believe in their government, and so they do.

The effectiveness of the sinister underground societies might best be illustrated by asking a few questions about the Kennedy investigation. Why was there never a recording made of any of Lee Harvey Oswald's statements during the 16 hours of police interrogations? Why did Oswald say to the media, "I never shot anybody," and, "I'm a patsy."? Why would the man responsible for planning and executing the most sophisticated assassination of modern times leave his gun and shell casings for police to find, walk downstairs and have a Coke before going home to get a pistol, kill a cop, then go to a movie instead of hiding out or trying to escape?

What did John Kennedy mean, ten days before his death, when he told a Columbia University audience, "The high office of President has been used to foment a plot to destroy the Americans' freedom, and before I leave office I must inform the citizen of his plight."? Who did he cause to worry?

Four years after the death of Kennedy, 18 witnesses in the case had died of one cause or another. A mathematician hired by the London *Sunday Times* in 1967 determined the odds of that happening were about 100,000,000,000,000 (one hundred *trillion*) to one. Since then, nearly 100 more have been added to the first 18, all of them somehow connected to the Kennedy assassination—doctors, investigators, witnesses from Dealey Plaza at the time of the murder.

Why was John Kennedy's brain "lost" during the investigation, precluding the benefit of autopsy results? Did the examination, in fact, prove the fatal bullet came from the famous grassy knoll and not the book depository? Why is all other investigative information locked away in some government time capsule?

Craig Roberts, a veteran law enforcement officer and sniper expert, exposed the truth about Kennedy's death in his book *Kill Zone: A Sniper Looks at Dealey Plaza*. He revealed convincingly *who* ordered the "execution," who manipulated the media, controlled the investigation, covered up the evidence, sealed the files and blocked the truth for 30 years. In summarizing the 1963 assassination plot, Roberts aptly described the direction of government in the 1990s:

> *By exposing the diabolical behind-the-scenes activities and secret histories of many organizations, both within and outside of the U.S. government, we have seen that murdering* [a president] *was considered little more than business as usual. The secret societies and councils that have emanated from the original Rothchild conspiracy . . . are the powers behind not only the U.S. government, but every major government in*

the world today. Their objective . . . is a one-world government that has dominion over all nations. Of necessity, this global entity must have a one-world monetary system, a global military police force, and a single anti-Christian humanist religion.

Interestingly, those "secret societies" were prophesied in *The Book of Mormon.* An eternal lesson on the "secret combinations" in Chapter 8 of Ether also reads with timeless admonition:

> *Behold, is there not an account concerning them of old, that they by their secret plans did obtain kingdoms and great glory?*

> *. . . and the people were kept in darkness, to help such as sought power to gain power, and to murder, and to plunder, and to lie, and to commit all manner of wickedness and whoredoms.*

> *For the Lord worketh not in secret combinations . . . and whatsoever nation shall uphold such secret combinations, to get power and gain, until they shall spread over the nation, behold, they shall be destroyed.*

> *It is wisdom in God that these things should be shown to you . . . and suffer not that these murderous combinations shall be above you, which are built up to get power and gain . . .*

> *. . . yea, even the sword of justice of the Eternal God shall fall upon you, to your overthrow and destruction if ye shall suffer these things to be.*
>
> *Wherefore, the Lord commandeth you, when ye shall see these things come among you that ye shall awake to a sense of your awful situation, because of this secret combination . . .*

> *For it cometh to pass that whoso buildeth it up seeketh to overthrow the freedom of all lands, nations and countries; and it bringeth to pass the destruction of all people . . .*

The description of "secret combinations" in *The Book of Mormon* is amazingly applicable to 20th century world politics. Contemporary secret combinations have resulted in the extermination of millions based on religion and ethnicity. They have gained control of governments, the media and monetary systems throughout the world. They have created wars, orchestrated economic depressions, and engineered genocide by design of famine, disease and societal decay. They have furnished deadly, mind-altering substances to the youth of nations and denigrated the significance of God. They have pitted races and religions against one another to weaken them all and make them submissive to an emerging United Nations world police force.

Karl Marx envisioned Utopia in socialism, and boasted, "My object in life is to dethrone God and destroy capitalism."

Lev Davidovich Trotsky denounced religion as "illogical primitive ignorance," and added, "There is nothing as ridiculous and tragic as a religious government."

Interesting, isn't it, that these icons of failed social and political ideology attacked the very basis for the most successful system of government in the world—religion and free enterprise?

Proponents of the New World Order are entrenched in high places and moving aggressively forward with their plan. Lieutenant Colonel James "Bo" Gritz, most decorated Green Beret commander in American history turned political activist, explains the "consipracy" within the U.S. Government:

> . . . *a spider web of "patriots for profit," operating from the highest positions of special trust and confidence, have successfully circumvented our constitutional system in pursuit of a New World Order. They have infused America with drugs in order to fund covert operations while sealing the fate of our servicemen left in Communist prisons.*
>
> *Hiding behind a mask of righteousness, this secret combination seeks to impose its own concept of geopolitical navigation, nullifying liberty as the hard-won birthright of all Americans.*

Their success depends on the perpetual ignorance, inaction and apathy of American citizens. The secret combinations cannot achieve the New World Order in the face of an armed citizenry—a nation armed not only with guns, as prescribed by the Founding Fathers, but with *knowledge* and *truth!* At the hands of a united "nation under God," the secret combinations " . . . *shall be destroyed* . . "

A religion that never suffices to govern a man, will never suffice to save him. That which does not distinguish him from a sinful world, will never distinguish him from a perishing world.

John Howe

Christianity is the companion of liberty in all its conflicts, the cradle of its infancy, and the divine source of its claims.

Alexis de Tocqueville

Chapter Thirteen:

From Such Turn Away

The scriptures and the teachings of Jesus Christ contain many references to the "last days" and the second coming of the Savior. Perhaps none is more powerful than Apostle Paul's prophecy in II Timothy 3:1-5:

> *This know also, that in the last days perilous times shall come.*
> *For men shall be lovers of their own selves, covetous, boasters, proud, blasphemers, disobedient to parents, unthankful, unholy,*

*Without natural affection, trucebreakers,
false accusers, incontinent, fierce, despisers of
those that are good,*

*Traitors, heady, highminded, lovers of
pleasures more than lovers of God;*

*Having a form of godliness, but denying the
power thereof: from such turn away.*

Paul's allusion to boasters, blasphemers,
trucebreakers, false accusers and traitors might well apply
to many 20th century politicians. Many important political
leaders of the nation swear to uphold and defend the U.S.
Constitution, then summarily put the oath aside. They
function, then, according to personal political ideology,
special-interest lobbying, profitable vote trading, hidden
agendas and "political correctness," but they ignore the
Constitution. Some of them believe the basis for American
government in 1787 can no longer apply as the basis for
government in a much larger modern, industrialized nation;
they purposely subvert the American political foundation.
Others have little idea of the *meaning* of the Constitution or
the proper role of government, and they function in
ignorance.

The concept is simple. The Constitution and Bill of
Rights were written to limit government. The limitations
were specific and clear. To exceed them was to violate the
Constitution. To violate the Constitution was to jeopardize
the principles of liberty, and would constitute an act of
treason.

The list of constitutional violations committed by the

various branches of the Federal Government is nearly endless. The Supreme Court, the Congress, the President, and nearly all facets of the federal bureaucracy have exceeded their authority at the high cost of impairing God-given liberty.

Does the Constitution need interpretation?

>*Congress shall make no law . . . prohibiting the free exercise . . .*

>*. . . the right of the people to keep and bear Arms shall not be infringed.*

>*. . . to be secure in their persons, houses, papers and effects . . . shall not be violated . . .*

>*. . . nor shall private property be taken for public use, without just compensation.*

>*Excessive bail shall not be required, nor excessive fines imposed . . .*

>*The powers not delegated to the United States . . . are reserved to the States . . .*

What is questionable about the meaning of these phrases from the Bill of Rights? An average high school student is capable of comprehending the words and their meanings. Why, then, has the Constitution and its companion Bill of Rights been raped and gutted and mutilated by a multitude of Supreme Court interpretations? "Interpretation" turns the simplistic into the complex, the explicit into the obscure. And it provides the *interpreter* with unlimited dominion over the intentions of the original creator (in this case, the *many creators* of the Constitution), so individual attitudes, social trends, societal mores, personalities and politics all become a part of the process. "Interpretation" is synonymous with "change."

The Founding Fathers never meant for "freedom of speech" to protect flag-burning or pornography. They would have dismantled a Supreme Court (or any branch of government) that favored abortion and homosexuality as quickly as they would have terminated one condoning murder and adultery. They would have risen in armed rebellion over Congress authorizing the privately-owned Federal Reserve to print and control circulation of the national currency. Federal officials would do well to spend less time interpreting the Constitution, and more time obeying it.

Corruption and degradation within our government has caused "perilous times," and has supported the disobedient and unholy, the traitors and those "without natural affection."

In the book of Genesis, Abraham begged the Lord to spare Sodom on condition that he would find ten righteous people. The Lord agreed. However, the ten could not be found. The cities of Sodom and Gomorrah were ultimately destroyed after two angels came to the house of Lot. The men of Sodom saw the angels and " . . . *compassed the house round, both old and young, all the people from every quarter. And they called unto Lot, and said unto him, Where are the men which came in to thee this night? bring them out unto us, that we may know them."*

Lot offered unto the men of Sodom his two virgin daughters so that they might " . . . *only unto these men* [the angels] *do nothing . . .* " The mob, consumed with lusting for the angels, refused. God destroyed the cities of Sodom and Gomorrah with "brimstone and fire" over their absolute compulsion for homosexuality and other displays of confirmed ungodliness. Lot and his two daughters—the only survivors—traveled away from Sodom to a place called Zoar.

Has our society not deteriorated to the level of debasement known in Sodom? Government has failed to improve anything with expensive social programs. The courts have added to the problem by waltzing with criminals, legitimizing abortion and sheltering homosexuals. Congress will remain impotent as long as the lobbying efforts of degenerates are more meaningful on Capitol Hill than the instructions of God.

Legislators have " . . . *a form of godliness . . .*" in the swearing of their oaths, but readily and consistently deny the power of it. *From such turn away!*

Would "ten righteous people" please step forth from the halls of Congress? How many are there, keeping their oaths and strictly adhering to the Constitution? Their numbers are not yet enough. There are too many *politicians,* who will do whatever it takes to be reelected, and not enough *statesmen,* who will do whatever it takes to uphold their sacred oaths of office.

In II Chronicles 7:14, God made a promise:

> *If my people, which are called by my name, shall humble themselves, and pray, and seek my face, and turn from their wicked ways; then will I hear from heaven, and will forgive their sin, and will heal their land.*

Let us be reminded again of the immortal words of the second president of the United States, John Adams:

> *Our constitution was made for a moral and religious people; it is wholly inadequate for any other.*

All the unholy political strategies in the world will not heal our land. Our "land" was founded upon Christian principles, and only by recommitting to those principles—the very essence of the Constitution—will our land be healed.

While just government protects all in their religious rites, true religion affords government its surest support.

George Washington

Next to the duty which young men owe to their Creator, I wish to see a supreme regard to their country inculcated upon them.

Dr. Benjamin Rush

Chapter Fourteen:

And a Little Child Shall Lead Them

Those determined to alter and weaken the Great American Experiment have employed specific stratagems to further their efforts. The most important of these, and perhaps the most effective, is the indoctrination of children.

Priorities in American education changed drastically during the 20th century. Socialists seized the opportunity to inject their own curricula and methods of instruction into the system. Most Americans saw the changes as "progress" in a maturing industrialized nation. No one objected noticeably as lessons on government procedures and principles were omitted. Parents passively acquiesced to Supreme Court rulings that turned the scholastic arena from religion-oriented to atheist-based. Most Americans did not know that key historical and political events were being rewritten or eliminated from the lesson books in the interest of promoting world unity. Instruction techniques and many classroom offerings promoted social "correctness" over academic achievement. Vulnerable young children became the victims of a massive and cleverly orchestrated purge of values and knowledge based on religious morality and historical fact.

The process was gradual as generations of eager young minds were shaped and prepared for interaction in a global society. Communications skills degenerated tragically, while sexual promiscuity and venereal diseases skyrocketed in tandem with increased emphasis on sex education. Emphasis on history, geography and math was sacrificed in deference to ultra-liberal "discussions" on popular environmental issues and attitudes about global socialism.

By the mid 1980s, a devastating offensive had been launched against traditional methods of public instruction— a crippling strategy called "Outcome-Based Education." Benign-sounding in name, this tactic of the socialists equates to injecting cancer cells into an already weak and ailing organ.

Outcome-Based Education (OBE) offers no incentive or requirement for achievement. There are no comparative standards. Students are allowed (even encouraged) to work at their own paces. Competition is out. No one fails. There are no right or wrong answers. Traditional methods (the very concept) of collecting a required number of units (or credits) for admission into college are disbanded. There are no tests. Grades have no relationship with knowledge or academic achievement. Factual academic subject matter is replaced with vague and subjective topics. The A-through-F grading system is discarded in favor of a series of check marks on a card. A student coming out of the OBE system will be influenced by acquired notions, values, attitudes, emotions, opinions and relationships rather than by knowledge of facts and objective information.

OBE is an effective method of "brainwashing." It is a tool designed to "program" a nation of bright young individuals into a mass of mindless followers who will not question or resist the sacrifice of American sovereignty upon the altar of one-world government.

Biblical references to a peaceful coexistence between enemies appear in Isaiah, chapter 11:

> *And the spirit of the Lord shall rest upon him, the spirit of wisdom and understanding, the spirit of counsel and might, the spirit of knowledge and the fear of the Lord:*
>
> *And shall make him of quick understanding in the fear of the Lord: and he shall not judge after the sight of his eyes, neither reprove after the hearing of his ears:*
>
> *But with righteousness shall he judge the poor, and reprove with equity for the meek of the*

earth: and he shall smite the earth with the rod of his mouth, and with the breath of his lips shall he slay the wicked.

And righteousness shall be the girdle of his loins, and faithfulness the girdle of his reins.

The wolf shall also dwell with the lamb, and the leopard shall lie down with the kid; and the calf and the young lion and the fatling together; and a little child shall lead them.

"Wisdom and understanding, the spirit of counsel," and "the spirit of knowledge" are prophesied as essential virtues, but no word is written of combining governments into a single world power. In fact, quite to the contrary:

And it shall come to pass in that day, that the Lord shall set his hand again the second time to recover the remnant of his people . . . from Assyria, and from Egypt, and from Pathros, and from Cush, and from Elam, and from Shinar, and from Hamath, and from the islands of the sea.

And he shall set up an ensign for the nations, and shall assemble the outcasts of Israel, and gather together the dispersed of Judah from the four corners of the earth.

This is hardly the description of a Utopian one-world order.

The degeneration of this nation's public school system merely serves as another indictment against federal intervention. Local schools should be managed locally—by local school boards, faculty and administration, and by parents. *National* education policies rob local officials of their ability to serve the needs of their respective constituencies, and eliminate the flexibility (freedom) to deal with *local* needs on a personal, productive basis.

In application, national education policies have turned neighborhood schools into centers for sex instruction, outlets for free condoms, resource libraries for anti-Christian theories on evolution, and forums for promoting deviant lifestyles and socialistic philosophies. At the same time, government has banned classroom prayer and other Christian influences. The result is obvious.

A few decades ago, student discipline problems may have included chewing gum in class, talking out of turn, or the occasional toss of a "spit wad." Contemporary schools face frequent incidents of vandalism, assault, drug abuse, gang crime, rape and even murder. Juvenile delinquents are not afraid of the consequences attached to serious crimes because the "system" teaches them that *they* are the victims of society—that they are not "responsible" for their misdeeds because they are too young, or they live in poverty, or their parents are divorced, or they can't cope, or any number of other reasons why it's okay for vicious young hoodlums to rob, rape and kill.

Dr. Stanton E. Samenow discusses the topics of free agency and societal malfeasance in his book *Inside the Criminal Mind*:

> *We must begin with the clear understanding that the criminal chooses crime . . . He rejects society long before society rejects him; he is victimizer, not victim.*
>
> *The present reform programs, which have given hardened criminals social and vocational skills without coming to grips with the way they view the world, are costly, useless, dangerous.*

Dr. Samenow points out that criminals very quickly learn how to manipulate the system for their own benefit because society will make excuses for them and their behavior. He quotes one minister who says, "This is so old, it's new. It's all in the Bible."

Samenow explains:

> *What he (the minister) meant was that the issues I've addressed here are as old as man himself—man's power to choose, free will, good versus evil, man's response to temptation, his courage or cowardice in the face of adversity.*

Dr. Samenow, a psychologist and criminologist, believes that choice, free agency, responsibility and old-fashioned biblical values are vital lessons that effectively preclude criminal behavior. Would it not be appropriate and beneficial, then, to teach these ideals in school?

Socialist-driven curricula have frayed the moral fiber within recent generations of young people. Misguided youth mature into vulnerable and misled adults. To return the progeny of the nation to a level of political principles and moral conviction embraced by the Founding Fathers will take a very long time. The only road there is built on a bed of Christian principles.

No Matter what theory of the origin of government you adopt, if you follow it out to its legitimate conclusions it will bring you face to face with the moral law.

H. J. Van Dyke

Chapter Fifteen:

With Wings As Eagles

The republic of the United States was founded on a wide range of religious influences. George Washington, as first president of the fledgling nation, was quick to recognize the existence and importance of all of them.

Presbyterians, of whom there were many among the Founding Fathers, recognized in the Adopting Act of 1729 the fundamental freedom of the Christian person as "liberty in Christ"—a precept that carried over predominantly into the U.S. Constitution. Washington addressed the Presbyterians with particular respect and gratitude:

> *While all men within our territories are protected in worshipping the Deity according to the dictates of their consciences; it is rationally to be expected from them in return, that they will be emulous of evincing the sanctity of their professions by the innocence of their lives and the beneficence of their actions; for no man, who is profligate in his morals, or a bad member of the civil community, can possibly be a true Christian, or a credit to his own religious society.*
>
> *I desire you to accept my acknowledgments for your laudable endeavors to render men sober, honest, and good Citizens, and the obedient subjects of a lawful government.*

To the United Baptists, Washington reiterated his commitment to unrestricted religious freedom:

> *. . . if I could . . . conceive that the general government might ever be so administered as to render the liberty of conscience insecure, I beg you will be persuaded that no one would be more zealous than myself to establish effectual barriers against the horrors of spiritual tyranny, and every species of religious persecution.*

By removing the "liberty of conscience" from the academic environment of the nation's young, the U.S. Supreme Court is guilty of the truest definition of "spiritual tyranny." To the Quakers, Washington expressed no willingness to compromise his convictions:

> *The liberty enjoyed by the people of these states of worshipping Almighty God agreeably to the consciences, is not only among the choicest of their* blessings, *but also of their* rights.

The President extended his blessing to Catholics:

> *. . . may the members of your society in America . . . as faithful subjects of our free government, enjoy every temporal and spiritual felicity.*

Washington addressed other denominations and congregations, but nowhere were his intentions for the nation's posterity made clearer than to the members of the Reformed German Congregation of New York:

> *The establishment of Civil and Religious Liberty was the Motive which induced me to the Field; the object is attained, and it now remains to be my earnest wish and prayer, that the Citizens of the United States would make a wise and virtuous use of the blessings, placed before them . . .*

The Constitution and the government it established has become increasingly roiled and confused during the last decades approaching the 21st century. That's because " . . *wise and virtuous use of the blessings . . .* " have been discarded and ignored.

The Constitution says nothing about education. The Founders, however, were devoutly committed to a system of public instruction that would guarantee preparation for young people in the guardianship of liberty. James Madison said, "A people who mean to be their own governors must arm themselves with the power which knowledge gives."

Dr. Benjamin Rush, perhaps the most learned of all the signers of the Declaration of Independence, believed the Bible and Christian doctrine should be parts of the curricula for all schools. Coupled as if married, the Bible and the Constitution would provide the instructional foundation for the successful perpetuation of the American Republic.

Shortly after the Constitution was ratified, the comprehensive study of its provisions was introduced into nearly all the nation's schools. Concerted efforts to teach the fundamentals of the Constitution as the basic law and political structure of the nation remained ongoing for more than a century. In many curricula, it was simply accepted as a normal part of American history classes.

During the second decade of the 20th century, however, attitudes about the most effective public instruction changed dramatically. A thing called "progressivism" was born, and quickly changed the focus of education away from traditional history, language and government classes. The National Education Association (NEA) determined that subjects lending themselves to "social efficiency" were more important. In 1918, the NEA released "The Cardinal Principles of Secondary Education," an official declaration which virtually ended study of the

Constitution in deference to current events. By 1930, little more than a mention of the U.S. Constitution appeared in most authorized textbooks.

As a result, the face of public involvement in government action is changed (reduced) to periodic dabbling during election years, and gross misunderstanding of the political structure of the nation is predominant. Too many voters think they elect representatives to bring home preferential "pork-barrel" favors. Millions have no conception of the proper roles and functions of federal, state and local governments. Elections are viewed as popularity contests between "personalities." Campaigns are run on the same basis. Citizens mistakenly believe a president is personally to credit or to blame for successful or failed policy. Congress is perceived as having the power to do whatever it wishes with the property of citizens. The Supreme Court is never challenged. The masses yield to self-empowered bureaucrats. A government of, by and for the people has evolved to a government of, by and for special interests.

Is it possible, then, that the Great American Experiment could fail? Might the greatest nation that ever graced the face of the earth crumble under the destructive forces of corruption, greed and abuse of power?

Yes.

We must remember the Founding Fathers made the Republic of America unique in that its constitution did not grant rights and liberties; it only protected those that were granted by the Creator. The Founders knew human nature and thought it prudent to restrain government, thereby restraining the natural temptation in humans to abuse positions of power. The "people" retained all powers not expressly delegated to the government.

The philosophies and principles of the Founding Fathers have all been forsaken. Each branch of government has found ways to authorize itself more power than can remain contained within its original confines. The Supreme Court has found explanations for their own rape and dismembering of the Constitution. Socialistic organizations operating under the cover of constitutionally-guaranteed freedoms have sought to dramatically alter the structure of the republican system.

The "separation of powers" principle has taken a beating by all three branches of federal government. The concept of liberty and rights originating with the Supreme Being has been traded for "interpretations" of freedom by the Supreme Court. Abandonment of the Founders' "gold standard" has led to unrestrained taxation, debt, inflation and government spending, not to mention an overall inflation rate of 821 percent since 1933. The American people have lost their understanding and appreciation for the constitutional principles installed by the framers of the founding documents.

So has the time come for American citizens, overwhelmed by the gloom-and-doom of it all, to throw up their hands in despair and resign? Are we beyond all hope?

No!

Those sentiments are reasonable. The future of America appears bleak. The U.S. Constitution *is* hanging by a thread. The liberty it was designed to protect is a fading, flickering light beyond an abyss of greed, manipulation, corruption and the dawning New World Order.

The temptation to give up, however, must be resisted at all costs. Americans must exhaust all peaceful means possible to "secure the blessings of liberty." If those fail, then more drastic measures must be employed. Every American citizen has a moral duty to his or her family—especially the children—to fight to preserve liberty and freedom. Citizens must also recognize their sacred obligation to defend God's laws and the eternal principles from which all "rights" were born.

The Constitution provides the mechanism necessary to restore the Founding Fathers' original intent. The distribution of powers has never been altered, except by arbitrary action. Therefore, the *people* still retain the ability to repair much damage through legislation in Congress. The Congress itself has every tool and weapon at its disposal to force an out-of-bounds Judicial Branch back into line. Appellate jurisdiction is controlled by Congress. The Senate must confirm presidential nominations to the Court. Congress also has the capability of returning states' powers and rights to their rightful place—the states.

The people have the power to remove senators and congressmen—even presidents—who behave as "activists" rather than elected representatives. It is also incumbent upon the nation's citizenry to study and become familiarized again with the principles of republican government established by the Founders. This knowledge must be used to elect legislators, governors, presidents, local officials and even school board representatives. Elected officials who misperform can be removed by recall, or at the next regular election.

Abraham Lincoln believed the key to sustained freedom lay in its own application:

> *Let* [the Constitution] *be taught in schools, in seminaries, and in colleges; let it be written in primers, in spelling books and in almanacs, let it be preached from the pulpit, proclaimed in legislative halls, and enforced in courts of justice. And, in short, let it become the political religion of the nation.*

Children must be taught not only the principles of liberty as outlined in the Constitution, but the laws of God that put them there. Any further attempt to separate the two will only accelerate the downward spiraling of American freedom.

The two most important solutions are perhaps the simplest.

First, no sensible person should depend on politicians in Washington, D.C., to "do it for you." The system is complex and corrupt. (That's largely what this book has been about.) The Federal Government has sold us out as free Americans. Too many of the "godless federalists" are mired permanently in the quicksand of selfish, dishonest politics. Too many of them favor the concept of the New World Order.

Don't depend on federal government to restore the Constitution. Instead, elect local and state officials who comprehend the Constitution and its tenets of freedom, who understand the proper role of government, and who will take seriously their oaths of office to "uphold and defend" God-given rights. By electing the right people to county and state governments, the nation can (and will) restore its Constitution, county by county, state by state.

Only a few local elected officials are necessary to pass and enforce laws reestablishing the Constitution as the Supreme Law of the Land. The Bill of Rights can be held absolutely inviolate, and transgressors of those rights can be arrested and charged with treason. The process only requires a board of county commissioners and a sheriff. A single *county* can reaffirm the provisions of the Constitution without spending a dime or firing a shot! And other counties will follow.

Secondly but not secondarily, the American public must once again recognize the importance of God in the process. George Bernard Shaw, a British philosopher and critic (even of Christianity), saw the value of Christian influence over matters of state:

> *After reviewing the world of human events for sixty years, I am prepared to say that I see no way out of the world's misery except the way that Christ would take were He to undertake the work of a modern statesman.*

Modern statesmen might take heart in the message from Isaiah 40:31:

They that wait upon the Lord shall renew their strength; they shall mount up with wings as eagles, they shall run, and not be weary; and they shall walk and not faint.

The political solution is a vain effort without the help of God. America's future is still in His hands; it is dependent upon our faith in Him. If we obey His law and commandments, and offer fair and just treatment to our fellow men, then perhaps God *will* bless America!

The End

God bless all of you for your dedication to God, Family, and Country.

Ronald Reagan

Bibliography

Allen, W.B. (Compiled and edited by), *George Washington: A Collection*, (Indianapolis, IN; Liberty*Classics*, 1988)

Barton, David, *America: To Pray or Not To Pray*, (Aledo, TX; Specialty Research Associates, 1988)

Benson, Ezra Taft, *An Enemy Hath Done This*, (Salt Lake City, UT; Parliament Publishers, 1969)

Benson, Ezra Taft, *The Constitution: A Heavenly Banner*, (Salt Lake City, UT; Deseret Book Company, 1986)

Berger, Raoul, *Government by Judiciary*, (Boston, MA; Harvard University Press, 1977)

Bork, Robert H., *The Tempting of America: The Political Seduction of the Law*, (New York, NY; Simon & Schuster, Inc., 1990)

Cord, Robert, *Separation of Church and State: Historical Fact and Current Fiction*, (New York, NY; Lambeth Press, 1982)

Dreisbach, Daniel L., *Real Threat and Mere Shadow: Religious Liberty and the First Amendment*, (Westchester, IL; Crossway Books, 1987)

Edwards, Tryon (Originally compiled by), Catrevas, C.N., Edwards, Jonathan, and Browns, Ralph Emerson (Revised and enlarged by), *The New Dictionary of Thoughts: A Cyclopedia of Quotations*, (Standard Book Company, 1961)

Eidsmoe, John, *Christianity and the Constitution: The Faith of Our Founding Fathers*, (Grand Rapids, MI; Baker Book House Company, 1987)

Evans, M. Stanton, *The Theme Is Freedom: Religion, Politics and the American Tradition*, (Washington, DC; Regnery Publishing, Inc., 1994)

James Version, King, *The Holy Bible*, (Nashville, TN; Thomas Nelson Publishers, 1984)

Long, Hamilton Abert, *The American Ideal of 1776*, (Philadelphia, PA; Your Heritage Books, Inc., 1976)

Mack, Richard I., Walters, Timothy Robert, *From My Cold Dead Fingers: Why America Needs Guns*, (Safford, AZ; Rawhide Western Publishing, 1994)

Morris, A.M., *The Prophecies Unveiled*, (Winfield, KS; The Courier Press, 1914)

Rice, Charles E., *The Supreme Court and Public Prayer*, (New York, NY; Fordham University Press, 1964)

Roberts, Craig, *Kill Zone: A Sniper Looks at Dealey Plaza*, (Tulsa, OK; Consolidated Press International, 1994)

Rossiter, Clinton, *Seedtime of the Republic*, (New York, NY; Harcourt, Brace & World, Inc., 1953)

Samenow, Dr. Stanton E., *Inside the Criminal Mind*, (New York, NY; The New York Times Book Co., Inc., 1984)

Siegan, Bernard H., *Economic Liberties and the Constitution*, (Chicago, IL; The University of Chicago Press, 1980)

Skousen, W. Cleon, *The Making of America: The Substance and Meaning of the Constitution*, (Washington, DC; The National Center for Constitutional Studies, 1985)

Smith, Jr., Joseph (Translated by), *The Book of Mormon: Another Testament of Jesus Christ*, (Salt Lake City, UT; The Church of Jesus Christ of Latter-day Saints, 1981)

Smylie, James H. (Edited by), *Presbyterians and the American Revolution: A Documentary Account*, (Philadelphia, PA; Presbyterian Historical Society, 1974)

Stedman, W. David and LaVaughn, Lewis G. (Edited by), *Our Ageless Constitution*, (Asheboro, NC; W. David Stedman Associates, 1987)

Walters, Timothy Robert, *Surviving the Second Civil War: The Land Rights Battle . . . and How To Win It*, (Safford, AZ; Rawhide Western Publishing, 1994)

Whitehead, John W., *The Freedom of Religious Expression in Public Universities and High Schools*, (Westchester, IL; Crossway Books, 1985)

Whitney, David C., *Founders of Freedom in America*, Vol. 1, (J.G. Ferguson Publishing Co., 1965, Dist. by Encyclopaedia Britannica Educational Corporation, Chicago, IL, 1971 ed.)

Wills, Garry (Edited with an introduction by), *The Federalist Papers by Alexander Hamilton, James Madison, and John Jay*, (New York, NY; Bantam Books, 1982)

Index

Editor's Note:

Rawhide Western Publishing is dedicated to the restoration and preservation of citizens' rights and freedoms as defined by the Founding Fathers in the U.S. Constitution and Bill of Rights. These, and only these, are the authorized laws of the land. The **RWP** mission is to serve as a conduit for the truth, to better inform the mainstream American public. We survive on no one's funding but our own. Therefore, we must make a small profit on our quality publications. We are prepared, however, to offer maximum discounts from retail prices on multiple book orders. We encourage every concerned citizen to become an important link in the information chain. You can help spread the word to those who don't already know what's happening to our American way of life. Use the order coupon in the back of this book. Speaking engagements with the authors may be arranged through **Rawhide Western Publishing.**
Write to: PO Box 327, Safford, AZ 85538.
Call: 1-800-428-5956.

DISCOUNT SCHEDULE

(Listed Prices Include All Shipping and Handling)

1 copy $14.95
2 copies (10% off) $26.30
3 copies (15% off) $37.53
4 copies (20% off) $47.44
5 copies (25% off) $56.05
10 copies (40% off) $90.30
20 copies (42% off) $170.00
30 copies (45% off) $240.00
50 copies (47% off) $380.00
100 copies (47% off) $750.00
200 copies (50% off) $1,360.00

**Order Yours Today! Sell Them for Profit at $12.95
or Give Them Away to Your Friends and Neighbors!**

Please send_____copies of *Government, GOD and Freedom*
Please send_____copies of *From My Cold Dead Fingers*
Please send_____copies of *Surviving the Second Civil War*
      (mix titles for maximum savings)
Enclosed is my check or money order for $_____; or
charge my_____VISA or_____MasterCard. My card Number is:
_____Expiration_____
Signature_____
Print Name_____
Mailing Address_____
City/State_____
Zip Code_____Phone(_____)_____

Rawhide Western Publishing

is very actively involved in the fight for personal rights
and liberties as guaranteed in the U.S. Constitution.

WE'LL HELP *YOU* FIGHT THE BATTLE
WITH THESE IMPORTANT BOOKS!

(1) *GOVERNMENT, GOD AND FREEDOM:*
A Fundamental Trinity
By Timothy Robert Walters and Richard I Mack

(2) *FROM MY COLD DEAD FINGERS:*
Why America Needs Guns
By Richard I. Mack and Timothy Robert Walters

(3) *SURVIVING THE SECOND CIVIL WAR:*
The Land Rights Battle . . . and How To Win It
By Timothy Robert Walters

Give Copies to Everyone You Know!!
**The key to winning back our Constitution is education and
awareness. Everyone must become informed.**

SEND THIS PAGE FOR QUANTITY DISCOUNTS

Detach and fill out reverse side, then mail to:
Rawhide Western Publishing, PO Box 327, Safford, AZ 85548

OR CALL:
1-800-428-5956